I Was
Born in Slavery

Other titles in the *Real Voices, Real History*™ *Series*

I Was
Born in Slavery

Personal Accounts of Slavery in Texas

Edited by Andrew Waters

John F. Blair, Publisher
Winston-Salem, North Carolina

Published by John F. Blair, Publisher

The paper in this book meets the guidelines
for permanence and durability of the
Committee on Production Guidelines for
Book Longevity of the Council on Library Resources

Front cover—Photograph of Sam Jones Washington, reproduced from
the collection of the Library of Congress, LC-USZ62-125350

Library of Congress Cataloging-in-Publication Data

I was born in slavery : personal accounts of slavery in Texas / edited
by Andrew Waters.
     p. cm. — (Real voices, real history series)
Includes index.
   ISBN 0-89587-274-9 (alk. paper)
  1. Slaves—Texas—Biography. 2. African Americans—Texas—Interviews.
3. Slaves—Texas—Social conditions—19th century—Sources.
4. Slavery—Texas—History—19th century—Sources. 5. African
Americans—Texas—Social conditions—19th century—Sources.
6. Texas—Biography. I. Waters, Andrew, 1970- II. Series.

E445.T47 I23 2003
305.5'67'0922764—dc21

                              2002151705

Book design by Debra Long Hampton

Composition by The Roberts Group

For my sisters Emily and Sara

Table of Contents

Introduction

The idea of Texas was built on a foundation of freedom. Today we understand the courageous group of men surrounded inside a dusty mission in San Antonio faced an overwhelming force to stand for this basic principle, fighting to their deaths while giving birth to a nation. The newly independent country attracted like-minded settlers, who flooded into this vast, often daunting territory seeking both economic opportunity and an escape from the increasing laws and regulations of the young United States. Frontiersmen such as James Bowie, David Crockett, and Sam Houston stood as icons for this proud, independent land.

The story shares elements with the American Revolution five decades earlier, but to this day Texas enjoys a unique, western image of independence. America believes the "Lone Star State" is a land of rugged individualists, men and women capable of standing on their own in the tradition of their heroic forefathers, their banner a bold sash of red, white, and blue accented by a single, defiant star. Texans, collectively dressed in cowboy hats and boots in our consciousness, are rightly proud of their unique heritage, often proclaiming their allegiance to their state prior to, or in the same breath, as their country.

These romantic images clash with a history of human bondage, and perhaps that is why Texas often escapes an association with the institution of slavery that other southern states must endure. It's true slavery had a relatively brief history in Texas, especially compared to states such as Virginia, the Carolinas, and Georgia, where slavery existed as a basis of the economic system for close to two hundred years. Slavery did not come to Texas until the 1810s and ended, of course, at the close of the Civil War. Despite this comparatively brief history, however, the institution played an important role in the state's early years. The majority of early settlers came to Texas from other southern states, and many brought their slaves with them. According to the 1850 census, 27.3 percent of Texas families owned slaves. By the 1860 census, that number had risen to 30.8 percent. As author Randolph B. Campbell notes in his study of Texas slavery titled *An Empire for Slavery: The Peculiar Institution in Texas* (Louisiana State University Press, 1989), these figures closely match the number of slaveholders in Virginia, where, according to census figures, 33.2 percent of Virginia families owned slaves in 1850 and 30.8 percent in 1860. "In this sense, then, slavery was as strongly established in Texas, the newest slave state, as it was in the oldest slave state in the Union," Campbell writes.

Certainly Ben Simpson's Texas was a not a land of freedom fighters, cowboys, and the open range. Simpson's Texas was a land of bondage. "My master he then got killed, and I became his son's property, and he was a killer," recalled the ninety-year-old former slave when interviewed in 1936. "After he comes to Texas, Boss, we never had no home, nor any quarters. . . . We wore chains all the time. Was never took off when we was at work. We either drug the chains or was snapped together, and at night we were locked to a tree to keep us from trying to run off. He didn't have to do that, 'cause we were afraid to run. We knew Master would kill us. Besides, he had already branded us, and they was no way to get that off."

Simpson was one of the hundreds of former Texas slaves interviewed by the Federal Writers' Project. Created in the midst of the Great Depression as part of the U.S. Works Progress (later Works Project) Administration (WPA), the agency provided work to jobless writers, editors, and researchers throughout the country. In Texas, as in the rest of the South, one of the Federal Writers' Project's major tasks was capturing the memories of former slaves, who were by then well into their eighties, nineties, and hundreds. Project administrators established a network of field workers to identify and interview these elderly men and women. In an age before tape recorders, the field workers were outfitted only with pencil, paper, and a list of questions. They transcribed the interviews in longhand and then typed them when they returned to regional offices.

Simpson's story parallels the history of Texas slavery in that he can recall being brought to Texas as a child or a young adult. Many of the former slaves interviewed in Texas recalled their journeys into the Lone Star State. "One mornin', we is all herded up. Mammy am cryin' and say they goin' to Texas but can't take Papa. He don't belong to them," remembered Josephine Howard, who was born on a plantation near Tuscaloosa, Alabama. "That the lastest time we ever seed Papa. Us and the women am put in wagons, but the men slaves am chained together and has to walk."

Betty Farrow, a ninety-year-old slave interviewed in Fort Worth, remembered the excitement and terror of the long journey from her birthplace in Patrick County, Virginia. "'Twas 'bout three yeahs befo' the war that Marster sold his plantation fo' to gwine to Texas. . . . I's 'members the day we'uns started in three covered waggins, all loaded. . . . We'uns travels from daylight to dark, 'cept to feed and rest the mules at noon. I's recollects comin' over the mountains. Lawd, we'uns was skeert some of the time. Sometimes the marster's wife and the girls screetched, 'cause we'uns could look down, down, and down. If the wagon tips over, whar we'uns go? But, thank the Lawd, we'uns never tips over. I's can't 'collects how long we'uns was on the way, but 'twas a long time and 'twarn't a celeb'ation towards the last."

The land these children and young adults found in antebellum Texas was an unsettled, rough country, and their memories often vividly recalled both the harshness of the land and the cruelty of those who enslaved them. Andy J. Anderson remembered the harsh treatment of an overseer named Delbridge left in charge after the property owner was impressed into the Confederate Army. "The first thing he [Delbridge] does am to cut the rations. . . . He half starve the niggers and demands mo' work, and he start the whuppin's. I's guess he 'cides to edumacate [educate] them. I's guess Delbridge went to hell when he died . . . I's don't think he go that far, though. I's don't see how the devil could stand him," recalled the ninety-four-year-old.

Anderson's recollections of brutality are not unusual. This is the third collection of slave narratives I have edited, and I found the Texans to be most forthcoming with accounts of brutality suffered at the hands of their masters. Indeed, one of the problems modern readers have with the slave narratives is that many of the former slaves recall their days under slavery with some degree of fondness. There has been speculation that the former slaves may have tempered their harshest memories. The interviews were conducted in the late 1930s, during a vast economic depression that was bringing what had already been difficult lives to an impoverished end. These elderly people had lived through one of our country's most tumultuous eras—slavery, Civil War, Reconstruction, Jim Crow and the rise of the Ku Klux Klan, World War I—and most had little to show for lives of suffering and hard work. Under these conditions it is perhaps understandable why these former slaves could view their days under slavery—childhood days unencumbered by the responsibilities of adulthood—as pleasurable, even joyful times.

Historians have suggested the context of the interviews also shaded the tone of the narratives. Some of the former slaves may have been apprehensive about revealing incidents of brutality to their interviewers, who were often white. This seems to be particularly true in the South and among former slaves who relied on whites for financial support. Historian Kenneth Stampp conducted a statistical experiment on the original narratives stored in the Library of Congress and found that slavery was remembered as a harsh institution by 38 percent of former slaves living in the North, compared to only 16 percent of those living in the South. Among narrators interviewed by whites, Stampp found 7 percent recalled slavery harshly, while 25 percent of those interviewed by blacks did so. Only 3 percent of the narrators clearly dependent on white support gave negative portrayals of slavery, but slavery was remembered negatively by 23 percent of those who seemed to be financially independent.

I'm not suggesting that sentiment is absent from this collection. "Old Missy, she sho's a good woman," recollected Gus Johnson, a ninety-year-old former slave living in Beaumont, of the woman who became his master after her husband died. "We have lots to eat, and if the rations run short we goes huntin' or fishin'."

"My white folks was pretty good to me and sorta picked me out," said Jeptha "Doc" Choice. "You see, if a nigger was smart and showed promise, he was taught how to read and write, and I went to school with the white children on the plantation."

You will find many memories in this collection that appear to depict slavery fondly, but just as many paint vividly brutal portraits of the inhumane system. "The old cap'n's a hard man, and the drivers was hard, too—all the time whipping and stropping the niggers to make 'em work harder," remembered Adline Marshall at her home in Houston. "Didn't make no diff'rence to the cap'n how little you is, you goes out to the field 'most soon as you can walk. The drivers don't use the bullwhip on the little niggers, but they play switch on us what sting the hide plenty."

I found the Texas narratives notable for the uniquely "western" lives lived by many of the former slaves. This is perhaps best exemplified by the account of James Cape, a remarkable man who worked as a cowboy both as a youth and after the war [not to mention the fact he served as a Confederate soldier]. In true cowboy fashion, he makes a point to tell his interviewer about a favorite horse. "I wants to tell you about my hoss," stated the centenarian Cape. "He has much sense as the man, 'cause he knows what to does. All I do am set on him. I warn't 'fraid to ride any place with him. The worster 'twas, the better I likes it. Yes, sir, I rides that hoss over all kinds of country, and we never gits hurt. One day, him and some other hosses am loose and playin' 'roun'. He was runnin' and steps in the hole and breaks his leg. We had to shoots him. I cried like the baby 'bout that." Cape also recalled hiring on with the outlaw Jesse James during a cattle drive to Missouri after the war, and who are we to debate him, especially when his reason for leaving the acclaimed bandit is so quintessentially Texan. "After three years I leaves, not 'cause I learnt he [James] outlaws, but 'cause I's lonesome fo' Texas."

Preserving these memories was one of the Federal Writers'

Project's greatest successes, and like most great achievements, the project required an astounding amount of work. Thousands of interviews were conducted throughout seventeen states. The composition of the individual narratives varied widely. Most were recorded in the first person but others were composed as factual third-person accounts. Some interviewers took great care with their subject, returning to a home several times for follow-up interviews. Other narratives comprise only a brief conversation, resulting in a finished narrative of only a page or two. Like most government projects, there were several levels of administration, resulting in duplication and mistakes. As a narrative made its way to a regional supervisor's office, it was typically edited numerous times. Multiple versions of the same interview were common. Today scholars acknowledge that many of the interviewers and editors involved in the project were subject to the same racial biases that affected others in the South—material that depicted whites most harshly sometimes was cut or changed substantially in the final drafts.

Eventually more than two thousand narratives were collected at the Library of Congress in Washington, D.C., under the title, *Slave Narratives: A Folk History of Slavery in the U.S. from Interviews with Former Slaves*. But the narratives, available only in the library's Rare Book Room or on microfilm for a $110 fee, remained a well-kept secret for decades. In 1972, scholar George P. Rawick compiled the Library of Congress narratives and published them as a series, grouped by state, titled *The American Slave: A Composite Autobiography*. The series sparked renewed interest in the narratives, and Rawick received letters from academics and researchers throughout the South informing him of "lost" or archived narratives that never found their way into the official Library of Congress collection. Rawick and his colleagues spent the next several years visiting these states in search of the missing narratives, finding some to be earlier versions of drafts that eventually made their way to the Library of Congress but many to be narratives that had never before been available to the public. Their quest resulted in the 1979 publication of a multi-volume supplement to the original *The American Slave*. This supplement contains hundreds of slave narratives that otherwise might still be languishing in storerooms.

Since then the narratives have appeared in various books and collections. My introduction to the material was through the collections of Belinda Hurmence, a writer and researcher in North Carolina. In the early 1980s, Hurmence became interested in the narratives as background for a historical novel she intended to write. However, she found the sheer volume of the Library of Congress holdings overwhelming and struck upon the idea of collecting the narratives in a smaller volume that would be less intimidating to an average reader. That idea resulted in her 1984 collection *My Folks Don't Want Me to Talk About Slavery*, containing twenty-one narratives of North Carolina slaves. Hurmence decided to include only narratives that were written in the first person, finding the versions told in the slave's own voice and dialect to be more engaging than the third-person accounts. She excluded the narratives of former slaves who had no clear memories of life under the slavery system, a necessary exclusion because many of those interviewed by the Federal Writers' Project were born just prior to or during the Civil War. She felt a clear recollection of slavery was crucial to the collection's relevance, and the formula was a success. That book has been in print ever since its publication and continues to find thousands of readers each year. Hurmence followed that first collection with a similar South Carolina collection, *Before Freedom, When I Just Can Remember*, and a Virginia collection, *We Lived in a Little Cabin in the Yard*.

I followed Hurmence's criteria in my first two collections of slave narratives, *On Jordan's Stormy Banks* (Georgia narratives) and *Prayin' to Be Set Free* (Mississippi narratives), finding no reason to stray from a formula that has remained successful for almost two decades. All of the narratives included in *I Was Born in Slavery* were written in the first person, most in heavy dialect, and contain memories of life under the slave system. Like Hurmence, I find the first-person narratives have an immediacy and intimacy the third-person accounts lack. These traits elevate the accounts from mere history to something that is ultimately more important—a voice speaking to us from the past.

As in past collections, dialect posed a central editorial problem. The writers and editors of the Federal Writer's Project took great care to preserve the former slaves' idiom, presumably feeling it was as important to preserve the subject's manner of speech as it was to preserve what they said. Unfortunately, the heavy use of dialect can make the narratives challenging to modern readers. I did not wish to correct all of the unusual spellings and abbreviations, because I also believe the manner of speaking is part of their story. I also did not want the dialect to hinder a reader's involvement with the material. Therefore, I attempted a balancing act, correcting the abbreviations and misspellings that seemed most irrelevant or unclear but leaving many abbreviations and the unusual syntax intact. Obscure words are often interpreted within brackets and editorial notes are provided for clarification. Some of these additions are my own; some were added by the original interviewers and editors. A small amount of repetitive material was cut, and occasionally material was rearranged for a better chronological sequence.

I selected male and female accounts equally because the sexes often had different experiences and perspectives of slavery. Creating an equal geographic distribution proved more difficult because the vast majority of Texas slaves resided in the eastern portion of the state, as did the majority of the state's population in general in the antebellum period. Prior to the Civil War, 93 percent of Texas's free population and 99 percent of its slaves lived east of a line extending from the Red River at approximately the 98th meridian southward to the mouth of the Nueces River. Substantial migration into western Texas did not occur until after the Civil War. Nevertheless, this was a huge territory. "The area of slaveholding, although covering only the eastern two-fifths of Texas, was as large as Alabama and Mississippi combined," writes Campbell. "Even without further expansion to the west, it constituted virtually an empire for slavery." From this empire emerged a rich deposit of material for Writer's Project field workers. Over 590 Texas slave narratives have now been located, the largest collection of any state. Almost all of these subjects lived in eastern Texas during slavery days, although some of those had migrated west by the 1930s.

With so many narratives to choose from, my challenge was not locating narratives that fit the criteria but selecting those that somehow offered unique perspectives on the Texas slave experience. This task was made somewhat easier by a unique feature. Many of the narratives in the Texas collection, unlike those from other states, contain a brief introduction and overview of the former slave's life. These introductions proved helpful in wading through the material, and I have included them here.

Nevertheless, readers may notice a repetitious quality to many of the narratives. This is primarily due to the predetermined list of questions from which the interviewers worked. Field workers were required to ask about home remedies and superstitions, among other topics that occur frequently.

The Texas revealed in these pages is, of course, not the Texas of freedom fighters at the Alamo or cowboys on the open range.

It is a place of brutality, suffering, and economic deprivation. It is not the mythic Texas. Nevertheless, the desire for freedom surely is just as strong among these African-Americans as it was for those heroic men inside the Alamo. "Master Davy told Sallie Freeman and a woman named Mary to get all the niggers in one place," recalled Lu Lee. "They rounded them up, and they came to the front yard. Mr. Davy stood on the porch and said he was going to read a proclamation. He started out to read, and he busted into crying, and his daughter had to read the paper. She read a paper and then talked it to us. She says, 'You is free mens and womens.' A man I knowed named George cried out in a powerful voice: 'Free, free, my Lord. Oh! Free, free, my Lord. Free, free, free, oh, my Lord. You will free me. And I was walking along one day, and thunder and lightning rolled over my head and brought on a dreadful day. Free, my Lord. Free, free, free! Free me, Lord—free, free, free.' I felt it roll over my head, too, and I cried. I thought on it something fine to be free. Better than religion." If Texas truly was built on a foundation of freedom, then Lu Lee and the other men and women whose narratives appear in this collection must be cast among those that played a crucial role in forming the Lone Star State. They remind us that freedom must be a requirement, not a privilege, for true independence to exist, perhaps creating a more accurate idea of Texas.

I Was
Born in Slavery

James Boyd

James Boyd was 107 years old when he was interviewed in 1937.
He was living in Itasca, in Hill County, Texas, when the interview
took place.

·|=··|=··|=··|=··|=··|=··|=··|=··|=··|=··|=··|=··|=··|=··|=··|=··|=··|=··|=·

I was born in Phantom Valley, Indian Territory, Oklahoma, in
an Indian hut. My father was name Blue Bull Bird, and my mother
was Nancy Will. She come with Santa Anna from Mississippi.
[Editor's note: Boyd refers to Antonio Lopez de Santa Anna, leader
of the Mexican military effort to crush the Texas rebellion in
1835-36. Boyd's reference to Mississippi appears to be a mistake, either in his memory or in the transcription.] My father
was raised in the Indian Territory. He had nine brothers and sisters, and they are all dead as far as I knows. I don't 'member
nothin' 'bout my grandpa and ma, 'cause I was lost from my
folks when I was a real little feller. A man the name of Sanford
Woolridge stole me while I was a-fishin' on the Cherokee River.
You see the white folks and the Indians had 'em a fight 'bout

that day. The white folks say it was just a small skirmish, but it sure seemed bad to me. I was 'way down on the creek, and I heard yellin' and shootin' and folkses runnin' and I slipt into some thickets right by the creek. By the bye, I didn't hear nothin' no more, and I slipt out. Then come a white man and he say: "Everybody kilt, nigger, and the Indians gwine kill you if they cotch you. Come go with me, and I won't let 'em hurt you." He wouldn't let me go to our hut, 'cause he say the Indians there and they gwine kill me sure. So I goes with him.

I split rails, drove oxen wagons and other jobs 'bout the place. I never did pick much cotton, and I never earnt much money. Iffen I did and was caught with any money it was taken 'way from me. Sometimes the boss give me a whuppin' 'cause he thought I had more money than I really had.

Us all cooked over a campfire, such as fish, 'possums, and bear meat. They ground corn with water mills. On Sunday, as a special treat, us had cottonseed meal to eat. It wasn't good, but when you're hongry anythin' eats very well. There was spinnin' wheels and looms, and the nigger women spun thread and wove cloth to make our clothes out of. I wore just what the rest did, cotton clothes in winter and summer, but us had some heavy cover clothes when it got real cold. I must-a been 'bout eighteen when I got my first shoes. They was brogan shoes, and they had brass tips on the toes. I sure thought I was fixed up to go to meetin' then.

I was 'bout thirty-six-years ole when the Freedom War broke. Marster allus teased me 'cause I didn't marry, and he allus tell my age. I fit [fought] in that Freedom War 'long side my Marster Sanford, and I got shot durin' the war. The bullet went through my breast and out my back, and there's a scar on my breast and back to this good day to show for it. I was wounded six months. The first battle I was in was at Halifax, North Carolina. Marster

Rube Hargrave was the captain. Us got the news of freedom and that the war was over when us was at Vicksburg, Mississippi. Most us niggers was 'fraid to say much, that is, the ole ones was, but the new ones thought the government gwine give them a span of mules and a farm, and they would be rich and wouldn't have to work. But they learned a lot these past fifty-six years. Us is sure slaves now to hard work, and lucky if we git work.

I been married eight times. My first wife was a Mexican. Her name was Martina, and I married her in 1869 down in Matamoras, Mexico. I went there after the Freedom War. Thought I could git more money there. Us had four children. She died and was buried in Matamoras.

I was kinder broke up and drifted back to Huntsville, Texas. There I married Emma Smith, and we only lived together 'bout a year and a half. Wasn't no chillun. Then I drifted to Fort Bend County, and there I married Mary McDowd. Us had two chillun. She died with the yellow fever and off I went for Burleson County. There I married Sally McDave, and she quit me after we had three chillun. Down in ole Washington County, I married Frances Williams, and us lived together 'til 1900. There was no chillun. Then I went to Austin after she died, and there I married Eliza Bunton in 1903. She died in 1911. Us had eight chillun. Then I comes to Hill County and marries Mittie Cahee in 1916. She quit me. In 1924, I married Hegar Price near Milford, Texas. We live together now, in Itasca, Texas. Us didn't have no chillun, but that don't matter 'cause I's the daddy of 'bout twenty-five already.

I sure did like my ole marster, but look out for mistis, she sure tough on niggers. There was 'bout 1600 acres in marster's plantation, and they had a nice big home. They would whup the niggers for stealin' and for fallin' behind with they work. One time I seed Hugh McIntyre and Earl Browning whup two niggers—women— to death. Us didn't have no jail, they didn't go to the trouble and expense of buildin' nigger jails. They just whupped us when they wanted to. I's seed lots of slaves chained. When they was movin' them and if the overseer was a bad-un, the niggers would run 'way, and then those kind of overseers would chain the niggers. Then, too, if they was gwine to sell a bunch of slaves, they would chain them together when they took them to market. On the march, if one of the chained ones fell down, the others lifted him up and drug 'em. On through creeks and all, they had to keep walkin' or git beat. If the water was deep, or the nigger little, he just swum or else he did the best he could. Didn't many drown, 'cause nigger is worth more 'live than he were dead.

There was some churches on the plantations, but us didn't have one. Aaron Nelly was sure a good preacher, and he could pray a fine prayer. They just buried the dead most anywhere where there was a good place—under a tree, on a hill, and like that. The white folks buried all their folks on their 'special family buryin' ground on the plantation. Sometimes they was buried in wooden boxes, and sometimes both white and black was buried just wrapped up. They wasn't no places to make things [caskets] like now and no graveyards. They did the best they could. They used to sing lots of purty songs, but I just can't 'member how they goes now. I never was no fine singer noways.

The slaves did run off and try to go north, but nigger steal-ers most offen got 'em, and then they would be sold again and maybe git worse hands holt of 'em. Most in general 'round our part of the country, iffen a nigger want to run away, he'd light out for ole Mexico. That was nigger heaven them days, they thought, but soon as the Freedom come, I thought I'd try it an' git me a rich Mex wife and live like a big bug, but all I got, I sure worked hard to git it.

In slavery, on our place, we worked all day Saturday, and sometimes on Sunday, if the crops was in a rush. The slave women sewed, washed, and ironed for themselves and their families on Sundays and at night by a brush fire. On Christmas we—both black and white—allus had a big dinner.

Marster wasn't much on presents and money, but we did have warm clothes and plenty to eat and a dry place to live, an' that's more than lots of the niggers have now.

Sometimes us'd have cornhuskings, and there would be a dollar for the one that could shuck the most corn in a certain time. Us'd have a big dance 'bout twice a year, on Christmas and sometime durin' the summer. When the white folks had their big balls, we niggers would cook and wait on the white folks and watch 'em dance, but we had lots of fun on the side. And sometimes the visitin' white gemmans [gentlemen] would give us clothes or money. But us didn't dare to keep the money. Now if it was prize money at a huskin' or for pickin' cotton, us could keep that money to buy medicine or somethin' we had to have.

When a slave was sick, there was some ole slave woman that made a practice of nussin' that helped with the sick slaves. If it was too bad, the white folks had their doctor come, and the marster doctored us with calomel and quinine. The ole women slaves used dewberry roots, snake roots, slippery elm root, rosin weed, and other herbs to doctor with.

The first year after the war of freedom, I punched cattle on a ranch in south Texas. I drove cattle into Kansas, over what the white folks called the Chisolm Trail. I worked lots with cattle for Marse Woolridge and was what they called a top hand. My real name was Scott Bird, and I was born in snow time in January, don't know the day. I just has my birthday on any Sunday in January that the ole woman can kill a chicken and have a cake. Got to have that. I drifted into Mexico from this ranch. I drove some cattle for the white man that I worked for. I married in Mexico and did different kinds of work there.

In Hill County, I's farmed, 'cause the cattle days, they done over wid. For twelve years, I worked for Marse Claude Wakefield, near Milford, Ellis County, Texas. But I lives in Itasca, Hill County, Texas, now. This ole man ain't due to live nowhere long. I's gettin' 'bout ready to cross the river. My name up in the Territory was Scott Bird, but after Freedom, I changed it to James Boyd 'cause I lived near Austin with a man named Boyd. I changed to his name 'cause iffen the white folks changed their mind and we wasn't no more free, then I'd have a good boss. I's gwine be 108 years ole in January 1938, iffen the Good Lord spares me that long. I's seen a heap o' this here earth and the people in it, but I tells you, sure is hard times now. Us is ole and crippled and iffen the white folks and the government don't help this chile, I don't know what he gwine do.

When they said we was free, all us niggers throwed our hats in the air and hollered. Ole Marse say, "How you gwine eat and git clothes and such?" And then we sure was scairt, and most of us stayed near our white folks long as they lived. When Marse Boyd got me to drive them cattle to Mexico, he tolt me he wasn't well no more and for me to sell the cattle, send him the money, and then git me a job down there 'cause he thought I could make more money there. I didn't so much like there, but my wife was them kind of folks and she didn't want to come to Texas, so I stayed 'til she died. No plantations was ever divided that I knows of, but there was lots of white men that give their oldest slaves some stock and a little patch of land, some more than others.

They was some mens in white clothes ride 'round some in our neighborhood down Austin way. They never bothered nobody that I knows of, but I didn't meddle 'em none. I voted the Democrat ticket straight like my white folks did. I didn't see no use doin' nothin' else, 'cause the white folks goin' do what they wants anyhow.

Lu Lee

*Lu Lee was born in slavery, somewhere along the Louisiana / Texas
state line, to the Cook family about 1848-49. She now resides at
1714 Flint Street, Dallas, Texas, with her granddaughter and
subsists on the old-age pension.*

Both my granny and grandpa came out of Africa. They didn't
know better than to love red. The mens come in a ship and showed
the red hankies [handkerchiefs] and fooled them onto the ship.
'Fore they knowed it, they was in the chains and don't see the
land no more. Davy Cook, my old master, was the owner of the
ship. Long as I 'member, the niggers called them men the "Red
Hankies."

Mr. Davy Cook was a northern man, and he brought my
granny and grandpa to the United States. They lived in the North
a long time, and they breeded more slaves, but I heard that he
didn't sell all the niggers. Some trouble come up, and they
refugeed into Texas. They never could tell whether I was born in
Louisiana or Texas. They was along the line, and they stopped,

and my mother went into the covered wagon, and I was born.

Mr. Davy set up near to Blooming Grove in Cook County, Texas, only they calls it Navarro County now. His brother, Henry Cook, was 'mongst the refugeers, and he set up nearby. Guess as how that's why they called it Cook County.

They built a big log house with four big rooms. They didn't have no shingles but covered the house with post-oak boards. They built little log cabins over and about the land for the niggers. Mr. Davy had lots of land, too. He had lots of slaves. Onc't he had over a hundred of them, but he sold them off down to fifty. Master had three boys and three girls. All those chilluns was by the first wife. Miss Helen was the second wife. She married bettering herself. She didn't never have nothing before. She got above herself and would have been worse if master didn't hold her down. Master was a pretty old man, and she was young. He was a good man, and we loved him. When he had company, all the little niggers think we got to lie down between his feet and pat and love his legs. He set a heap of store by us, and he didn't believe in the overseers and the slave drivers. He wouldn't even have a patteroller on the place.

I had three brothers and three sisters. I only got one brother left now. When I was a real little girl, my dada, Alec Cook, wanted to marry one of Thurman's niggers—a gal named Caroline. Well, Mr. Davy Cook won't let him 'cause my mother is right to her time with the last baby. So my paw ran off and went down in the bottom lands and lived in a cave for three years before they found him. He lived right well, and the niggers knew where he was, but Mr. Davy don't know. He killed wild hogs, turkeys, and deers, and other meat and had just great big boxes of dried meat put up in that cave. Mr. Davy tried to run him with the bloodhounds, but when he went away he went through the prairie land and stepped all the way in fresh cow mess. It's a sho' way to keep dogs off your trail, 'cause it smells just like the grass. After the Civil War, my dada married Caroline Thurman.

My mother just said to my paw, "Go ahead if you don't like me no more." My mother took soon to have the baby, and she was bad in time, and Mr. Davy had to get Dr. Wheeler to her. She died when the baby was about three weeks old, and Dr. Wheeler took the little girl to pay for the bill. Dr. Wheeler and his wife didn't have no chillun, and they named the girl Sara and raised her in Waco.

I was real little, and I went to my aunt's cabin to live. The chilluns fought me and grabbed the vittles 'fore I could get any. I cried and got so puny and beat up that the white folks had to take me to live in the house with them. I slept in a one-legged bed. They made it by nailing planks along the wall and setting up a leg in the middle of the end pieces.

We all lived real well. Master raised plenty. He had orchards of fruit, and he raised cotton, corn, oats, and rice in the spring places. They hadn't ruined the land with them deep plows then, so the land all wash away. The prairies were full of prairie chickens, and the woods just full of every kind of wild game. When they see a wild cow that has a good bag, they cut her off from the herd and bring her to the lot and tame and milk her. But for vittles, we never wanted

Just three miles from the place was the Fifty Mile Thicket, and it was full of every kind of varmint and panther. The prairies were full of wolves and varmints. Miss Helen used to make my sister and me herd sheep in the prairies, and we was mortal scared of the wolves, panthers, and wild cattle. We wasn't scared of the big droves of wild horses, 'cause they run away if they see you. We kept big shepherd dogs with the sheep, but once we were herding the sheep, and we seen the wolves come down and grab a big, good-sized calf in small time.

Every day we use to see the Indians pass the house. They tied they babies on jennies and jacks. They lived on the prairie. Some had tents, and some had wagons. Sometimes they wore clouts [an article of clothing resembling a diaper], and I have seen them without nothing. They seemed right-nice folks. Leastways they didn't bother nobody. I seen the sojers [soldiers] come and drive them away to the frontier. They just herded them off in a hurry. One little Indian boy about six or seven that had been sick couldn't keep up with the way the sojers were driving them and gave out. My master found him lying down, 'cause he was so give out. He brought him home on his horse and gave him to the niggers to raise. He grew up and married one of my aunts. But there was something that always kept him a Indian. They was curious folks, but I don't know what they was nicer than white folks.

Now the animals: the deers and the panthers and game went off following after the Indians. Animals like the way Indians smell better than any other people. Panthers would jump on white folks and niggers, but not on Indians. They always hung around where the Indians were camped. Most of the prairie chickens went looking after the Indians on the frontiers.

Old Master David wouldn't let Miss Helen whup us or work us too hard. We used to play a lot. We used to play a ring game where we sang:

> Ring around the rosie
> Squat little josie.

We made mud pies and shuck dolls. There was a dollhouse we went into to play. We played with the white chilluns. I used to hear Master David call the chilluns and say, "You got your school books out there?" If they say, "Yes," then he tells them,

"Bring your books in the house, and then you can go back out and play."

But the thing we chilluns liked best was hunting for babies. The old granny women used to tell us that they found the babies in the hollow logs and in holes in the ground. We would go in the woods and look in the hollow logs and dig in all the stump holes. We would come back and say we didn't find no babies. They told us we didn't dig deep 'nuf. We dug our little selves crazy. One day we was hunting for babies, and we come up by a hollow log, and we found a baby fawn. The old mammy deers would sometimes run the fawns so hard that they would lie down and sleep like they was dead. This fawn was sound asleep, and we picked him up. When the old deer come up, the dog chases her off. We thought we had just found a baby deer instead of a folks' baby, and we were proud as Satan. We took the fawn home, and he grew up to follow like a dog.

When Old Man Davy had company he would call us in to sing for them. His special song for us was:

> Way down is the good old Daniel,
> Way down is the good old Daniel,
> Way down is the good old Daniel,
> We live in the Promised Land.

> By and by,
> By and by,
> We will go there to see him.
> We will go there to see him.
> We will go there to see him.
> We will go there to see him,
> And live in the Promised Land.

We didn't ever hear no preaching on the place at all. But we used to have prayings in the different cabins. They sang at the prayings. I never did prefess religion though, 'til I was 'bout eighteen years old. They used to sing "Amazing Grace" and a real pretty tune called "Pity Lord:"

Show pity, Lord.
Oh Lord, forgive.
Show pity, Lord.
Oh Lord, forgive
And let every penitent sinner live.

We didn't know nothing 'bout Sundays 'cept that was the day the niggers didn't go to the fields, and we washed and ironed our clothes. We made our clothes—leastways the women did. There was a loom house made out of logs, and there was looms and spinning wheels. Two women, Elizabeth and Sue, spun all the time. We dyed clothes with things out of the woods.

I remember when folks died, they built plank coffins and lined the inside with plain white cloth and the outside with black. They didn't have funerals in them days—they just buried the folks in a burying ground we had.

Mr. Davy was a powerful religious man, though. He used to let us have dancing and singings on Saturday night. Then we had cornshucking parties. At the dances, they used to have men with fiddles, and they hollered out, "Get your partners for the ring dance." Then they had 'nuther dance where they have dancing up the sides from head to foot and prancing back. I forgets a lot about it. But they used to dance to a song called "Black Jack Grove." Master Davy said it was wrong to dance but said, "Seek your enjoyment. Niggers got to pleasure themselves some way."

The niggers didn't use to marry 'nuther. The master would

hold a broom up and have the bride jump over it, and then he held it a little higher for the groom to jump. When they did that, he said, "Salute your bride." And that was all there was to it.

There was a Carrol nigger wanted one of master's gals, and Colonel Carrol told him to ask master. He come up and talked to master 'bout it, and Mr. Davy said he didn't like to stand 'twixt nobody, not even niggers, and so they married them. That nigger would get a pass and come over and stay with he gal. Then he would say, "I am sorry, but it is that certain time, and I got to go."

Zeke Bosman was the only overseer we ever had. He was on the place, and he spoiled a colored girl. Master found it out when she had a baby. He put her off in a house by herself and wouldn't let her even see her paw and maw. He ran Zeke Bosman off the place.

When women had babies, they had old granny women on the place to look after them. They stayed in bed three days and got up on the fourth. But if they had a bad time, they let them stay in bed four days. The women who had nursing babies did work around the house or in the spinning rooms, so they be where they can suckle the babies. For the babies, the granny women give them watermelon tea [hot water poured over watermelon seeds and left to steep] to make they kidneys act. They give them catnip to break out the hives on them.

For other sicknesses, we got herbs out of the bottom land. There was black jack poultices for pains in the side and black haw leaves to make tea out of for the fevers. For a bad cold, we would take a hog hoof and parch it, and then pour hot water over it and make a tea. That was a sure cure for colds and high fevers.

I have known two women that got pregnant and didn't want the baby. They unfixed themselves by taking calomel [chamomile] and turpentine. In them days, the turpentine was strong, and ten or twelve drops would miscarry you. But the makers found what it was used for, and they changed the way of making turpentine. It ain't no good no more.

They used to take indigo to unfix themselves. We raised indigo in the garden for bluing the clothes. After the bloom would drop off, we would take the stalk and beat it up and soak it in water, and the blue would settle to the bottom just like starch. Then when you drained the water off and dried it, you had bluing.

One day Miss Helen said to me, "Them folks up North going to try to take our niggers. You going with 'em?" I said, "No'm, Miss Helen, I ain't going no place." I didn't know what 'twas all about.

Right at that time, I was eleven years old. They put me on the stile block. They called it the stile block 'cause it was three steps high. Mr. Henry Cook, Mr. Davy's brother, bought me. Mr. Henry was a good man, but I don't think he had all that belonged to him. He warn't near as smart as Davy, and he ain't as religious. He was a Hard-Shell Baptist, though. Miss Polly, his wife, was a good woman. They had seventy-five or eighty niggers, and they was fair-to-good fixed. They house is standing down there today, near to Blooming Grove.

I was working height then, and I went to the fields to hoe and pick cotton. But they warn't hard on they niggers. You heared powerful talk of the war that was heading that way. And I seen straggling sojers going to whup the Yankees.

Mr. Jim and Mr. Bill, Master Davy's boys, went off with the Confederate Details. For a long time they was to the war. The Details didn't like the Cooks on account of them being from the North. Master Davy had to go down in the bottoms and live in a cave, just like my dada. The niggers kept him hid and kept him fed, and they never mumbled out what they knowed.

The Ku Klux and the patterollers was all around and doing meanness. They were just as ornery and mean as the policemen are now. They never did nothing that amounted to nothing in they life, so they think they is smart big mens when ten of them jump on a poor nigger and beat the life out of him. Niggers had to lay might' low. Their life warn't worth a five-cent piece. The conscripters was going over to the country, too. What I says is that folks like that ought to be taught up better than such carrying-on. Hitting them on the head won't do no good. God made all of them, and they ought to be learned the good, kind ways of living.

The Federals come down in that country. We heared they was bad folks, but they seemed right gentle-like, but for taking your horses and mules. They camped at a place near Raleigh. They took a horse away from my uncle and one from my brother, and they took some mules from some mens I knowed.

I was over to Master Davy's house to see my grandmammy. She said there was a paper every man must read that the Federals done brought to that country.

Master Davy told Sallie Freeman and a woman named Mary to get all the niggers in one place. They rounded them up, and they came to the front yard. Mr. Davy stood on the porch and said he was going to read a proclamation. He started out to read, and he busted into crying, and his daughter had to read the paper. She read a paper and then talked it to us. She says, "You is free mens and womens." A man I knowed named George cried out in a powerful voice:

"Free, free, my Lord. Oh! Free, free, my Lord. Free, free, free, oh, my Lord. You will free me. And I was walking along one day, and thunder and lightning rolled over my head and brought on a dreadful day. Free, my Lord. Free, free, free! Free me, Lord—free, free, free."

I felt it roll over my head, too, and I cried. I thought on it something fine to be free. Better than religion.

That night the niggers had a big cornshucking. They set up

torches and poured tallow in bottles around twisted cloth and put them on posts. They lit them all up and made a grand sight. They drank whiskey and danced, and they sang:

Dram, dram, dram,
Old Master David,
Old Master Henry.
Dram, dram, dram.
Oh, bum-a-licha, bum-a-licha, bum, bum.
Oh, bum-a-licha, bum-a-licha, bum, bum, ho!

I went back to Master Henry's house, and he said he was going to take me and my sister to the free state of Brazil where they could keep slaves. I told my sister we run away to go to my grandmammy's. We got on the prairie, and some wild cows chases us, and we clumb a tree. We had to stay there all day and all night. The next day, a uncle of mine was coming along the way driving some cattle, and we called him. He went after some white mens, and they come and got the steers away from the tree. So we went on over to my grandmother's.

There was talk of forty acres and a mule for the niggers. They fooled them on that. They say the Yankees was willing, but the folks in the South wanted to starve the niggers out. The patterollers was worse than ever. They shot and killed Johnny Hines, a white man I know. They killed Jim Cook, Master Davy's boy, down on Jack's Branch. They said he said things he hadn't ought of. Master Davy sent after him and brought him home, and they buried him there, but they didn't have no funeral. They killed a nigger boy named Henry, just 'cause he wouldn't go off with some cattlemen.

I went to work for Mark Burgess at Raleigh and worked there many a year. I married a Caldwell nigger when I was twenty-one.

He wasn't much good. We had one child. He sold oats and corn that didn't belong to him and got in trouble with the law. He had to leave. He slipped back to see me and asked me to go with him, but I couldn't. Someone told on him, but he had a fast horse and got away. I was glad 'cause I ain't seen so much in the law to think they are any better than them they chase.

I married again to a man named Will Green. He wasn't much good neither. We had three chilluns. He was jealous of me. But I never carried on in my life. Two of my chilluns died when they are babies.

I learned to be a granny woman. I got licenses from seven doctors. I birthed many chilluns. I always tell the women to set up on the ninth day to get their strength rightly.

Tucker Lee was the name of the last man I married. I guess I thought more of him. He was good, and then not much good neither. He ran away with another woman. The brother of that woman came to me and told me he was going to kill him. I talked him out of it. I said, "He is hurting himself. Maybe he will come back someday."

A few years later, I am working at the house of the woman that raised Tucker. The undertaker from Tyler [Texas] phoned this lady and asked if she knew Tucker Lee. She said, "'Course I do." He asked her to pay for his burying, 'cause he is dead. She said, "I wouldn't give a nickel on his heart." I told her she didn't have a heart. I sent ten dollars, 'cause that was all I had. I knew he had to be buried, 'cause he couldn't just lay on top of the ground.

I cooked in the government training school down at Blooming Grove and saved my money to send my granddaughter to college. But she got married, and I got old. The ten dollars I get from the government every month ain't a lot, but it helps me along. At least I don't starve. I'm through now with everything, and I'm ready to die and be done for all.

James Cape

James Cape, centenarian, now living in a dilapidated, streetless shack located in the rear of the stockyards, was born a slave to Mr. Bob Houston, a large ranch owner in southeast Texas. His has been a colorful life, with his parents coming direct from Africa into slavery. He spent his youth as a cowboy, fought as a Confederate soldier, was wounded in one of the battles and still carries an ugly shoulder scar. He hired as a cowboy to a Mr. Ross, who later proved to be a cattle rustler, from whom he escaped after a long cattle drive to Kansas City. Later he unknowingly took a job with an infamous outlaw, Jesse James, for whom he worked three years in Missouri on the James farm. Homesickness caused him to come back to Texas. He went to work in the Fort Worth stockyards, working until his health forced him to retire in 1928. Lacking documentary proof, we assume that Cape must be about one hundred because he should have been twenty or more to have participated in the Civil War, which began in 1861.

I's born in yonder southeast Texas. I don't knows what month or the year fo' sho', but 'twas more than a hundred years ago. My mammy and pappy was born in Africa. That's what they told

James Cape

me. They was owned by Marster Bob Houston. Him owned the ranch down there where they have cattle and hosses. There's where I's born.

When I's old 'nough to set on the hoss, they learnt me to ride, tendin' hosses. 'Twas the first work that I do that I can 'members. When I's old 'nough, I works herdin' hosses and helps drives them, here, there and ever'wheres. 'Cause I good hoss rider, they uses me all the time gwine after hosses. I goes with 'em to Mexico. Yes, sir, we crosses the river lots of times gwine after hosses. I's never been thrown off the hoss after I learnt to ride, and I have gone lickety-split over the rough ground chasin' critters.

The worst time fo' trouble am when there am a storm and the critters am in the open, and they wants to stampede. That's when the rider had to ride to keeps the critters' minds off of the storm. You had to sorta keeps them movin' hidder and yonder [hither and yonder], sorta keeps them fussed up. I 'members once when we was a drivin' 'bouts two hundred hosses no'th'ards [northwards], they was a bad hailstorm comes into the face of that herd. Well, that herd turns and starts the other way. There was five of us riders, two goes on one side, two on the other side, and I goes in the lead. We had to keeps them from scatterment. I have to ride like lightnin' fo' to keeps 'head of them. Do you knows what happens to this nigger if my hoss stumbles? Right there's where I would still be. I stays in the lead and gives 'em the leader. You knows the critters had to have their leader. The other mens keeps 'em from scatterment, and we saves all them hosses. Marster gives me a new saddle for givin' them a leader.

I wants to tells you about my hoss. He has much sense as the man, 'cause he knows what to does. All I do am set on him. I warn't 'fraid to ride any place with him. The worster 'twas, the better I likes it. Yes, sir, I rides that hoss over all kinds of country, and we never gits hurt. One day, him and some other hosses am loose and playin' 'roun'. He was runnin' and steps in the hole and breaks his leg. We had to shoots him. I cried like the baby 'bout that.

One day, Marster Bob comes to me and says "Jim, how would you like to join the army?" You see, the war had started. I says to him, "What does I have to do?" And he says, "Tend hosses and rides them." I's young then and thought 'twould be lots of fun, and I says, "I would like to go." So the first thing I knows, I's in the army away off east from here, somewhere this side of St. Louis in Tennessee, Arkansas, and other places. I goes fo' Doctor Carrol.

After I gits in the army, 'twarn't so much fun. Tendin' hosses and ridin' and ridin' 'twarn't all I does. No, sir, I have to do the shootin' and gits shot at. One time we stops the train, takes Yankee money and lots of other things, and goes on. That was 'way up the other side of Tennessee.

You's heard of the Battle of Inpen'ence [Editor's note: Cape refers to a battle near Independence, Missouri. In the three-day affair, which took place October 21-23, 1864, Brigadier General John S. Marmaduke's division of the Confederate Army of Missouri engaged Union cavalry led by Major General Alfred Pleasonton.] That's where we fights fo' three days and nights. I's not tendin' hosses that time. They gives me a rifle and sends me up front fightin' when we warn't runnin'. We does a heap of runnin' and that suits this nigger. I could do that better than advance. When the order comes fo' 'treat [retreat], I's all time ready. I could does that better than any of 'em. I gits shot in the shoulder in that fight, and the Yankee mans kills lots of our soldiers, takes lots of 'em. We lose lots of our supply, just leave it and runs. There was 'nother time we fights two days and nights. The Yankee mans was bad that time, too. They kills lots, and we had to runs through the river. I sho' thought I's gwine to git drowned.

If I had to goes 'nother foot, I would not be here now. That's the time we tries to gits in St. Louis, but the Yankee mans stops us.

I's free after the war, and I goes back to Texas. I goes to Gonzales County and gits a job doin' cowboy work fo' Marster Ross, herdin' cattle. There's where I's lucky fo' not gittin' in jail or gits hanged. 'Twas this-a way—I's in the town, and the man Ross comes to me and says, "I understand that you's a good cowhand." I said, "Yes." He hires me and takes me 'ways out. 'Twarn't no house fo' miles. We comes to the ranch with cattle, and I goes to work. After I workin' awhile, I wonder how come they bring in such fine steers so often. Most of the critters on that ranch was steers. I says to myself, "Marster Ross must have heaps of money fo' to buys all them steers." They pays no 'tention to the raisin' of cattle, just bring 'em in and drives them away after they gits lots at the ranch.

One time Marster Ross and six mens had been gone a week. When they comes back, one of them was missin'. They had no steers that time. I hears them talkin', and they says 'bout gittin' fusterated [frustrated], and how the one man gits shot by the peoples that chases them. I says to myself, "What fo' they's been chased? What they been doin'?" I 'members Marster Bob Houston tells 'bout cattle rustlers, and how they gits hanged when they gits caught. I says, "Ho, ho, that's how come them fine steers, and that's why they gits chased." I knows then that I have to leave that place, 'cause if the owner of them fine steers finds where this place am, we all gits hanged sho'.

Hows to gits away, there's a puzzlement. I's a way out where there's no house fo' I don't know how far. I's not know which way to goes. I keeps gittin' skeeter [more scared]. Ever' time I see somebody a-comin', I's sho' it's the law. Marster Ross often drives the cattle north, and I says, "That's the way I gits outer here." Next time I meets him I says, "Marster Ross, I's good hand at the drive?" Old Marster Bob says I's the best hand he has. "I's like to goes with you next time you goes north. I's like to see that country." He says, "Jim, you can go, we needs good hands on the drive."

'Twarn't long after that 'til we starts the drive north. We drives and drives them critters. Then we gits to Kansas City. After Marster Ross gits shut of the critters, he says to us, "We will rest fo' coupla days, have a good time, then we starts back." I says to me, "Not this nigger."

I sneaks away and was a-settin' on the bench front of a place when 'long comes a white man. He's tall, had dark hair, and was a fine-lookin' man. He says to me, "Are you a cowhand?" I tells him, "I is," and told him how I worked for Marster Bob. He says, "I wants a hand on my farm in Missouri." I tells him, "I wants the job pow'ful bad." He says, "Come with me." That man tells me his name was James, and he takes me to his farm where I tend to cattle and hosses for three years. He pays me well. He gives me mo' money than I earns. I learnt afterwards his name was Jesse James, and that he was the outlaw.

After three years, I leaves, not 'cause I learnt he outlaws, but 'cause I's lonesome fo' Texas. That's how come I comes to Fort Worth, and here's where I's stayed ever since. I gits job workin' fo' the cattlemans. There warn't any stockyards then. After they's built, I gets work there and work there 'til 'bout fifteen years ago. Since that time, I's work first one place and then another, doin' little work fo' the white folks, 'til five years ago I's not able to work. I now gits pension from the state. They pays me fifteen dollar ever' month. I's married 'bout forty years ago to a woman that had eight chilluns. We sep'rated 'cause them chilluns cause arguments. I can fight one, but not the army. I's not seen them since and have no livin' rel'tives that I knows of.

Betty Simmons

Betty Simmons, one hundred or more [years old], was born a slave to Leftwidge Carter in Macedonia, Alabama. She was stolen when a child, sold to slave traders, and later to a man in Texas. She now lives in Beaumont, Texas.

I think I's 'bout a hunnerd and one or two year old. My papa was a free man, 'cause his old massa set him free 'fore I's born and give him a hoss and saddle and a little house to live in.

My old massa when I's a chile, he name Mr. Leftwidge Carter. When he daughter marry Mr. Wash Langford, Massa give me to her. She was call Clementine. Massa Langford has a little store, and a man call Mobley go in business with him. This man brung down he two brothers, and they fair clean Massa Langford out. He was ruint [ruined].

But while all this goin' on I didn't know it, and I was happy. They was good to me, and I don't work too hard, just gits in the mischief. One time I sho' got drunk, and this the way of it. Massa have the puncheon of whiskey, and he sell the whiskey, too. Now, in them days, they have frills 'round the beds—they wasn't naked beds like nowadays. They puts this puncheon under the bed, and the frills hide it. But I's nussin' a little boy in that room, and I crawls under that bed and drinks out of the puncheon. Then I poke the head out and say "Boo" at the little boy, and he laugh and laugh. Then I ducks back and drinks a little more, and I say "Boo" at him 'gain, and he laugh and laugh. They was lots of whiskey in the puncheon, and I keeps drinkin' and sayin' "Boo." My head, it gits funny, and I come out with the puncheon and starts to the kitchen, where my aunt Adeline was the cook. I just a-stompin' and sayin' the big words. They never lets me 'round where that puncheon is no more.

When Massa Langford was ruint, and they goin' to take the store 'way from him, they was trouble, plenty of that. One day Massa send me down to he brother's place. I was there two days, and then the missy tell me to go to the fence. There was two white men in a buggy, and one of 'em say, "I thought she bigger than that." Then he asks me, "Betty, can you cook?" I tells him I been cook helper two, three month, and he say, "You git dressed and come down three mile to the other side of the post office." So I gits my little bundle, and when I gits there he say, "Gal, you want to go 'bout twenty-five mile and help cook at the boardin' house." He tries to make me believe I won't be gone a long time, but when I gits in the buggy they tells me Massa Langford done lost ever'thing, and he have to hide out he niggers for to keep the credickers [creditors] from gittin' them. Some of the niggers he hides in the weeds, but he stole me from my sweet missy and sell me so them credickers can't git me.

When we gits to the crossroads, there the massa and a nigger man. That another slave he gwine to sell, and he hate to sell us so bad he can't look us in the eye. They puts us niggers inside the buggy, so iffen the credickers comes along they can't see us.

Finally those slave spec'lators puts the nigger man and me in the train and takes us to Memphis. When we gits there, they takes us to the nigger trader's yard. We gits there at breakfast time and waits for the boat they calls the *Ohio* to git there. The boat just ahead of this *Ohio*, Old Captain Fabra's boat, was 'stroyed and that delay our boat two hours. When it comes, they was 258 niggers out of them nigger yards in Memphis what gits on that boat. They puts the niggers upstairs and goes down the river far as Vicksburg, that was the place. Then us gits offen the boat and gits on the train, and that time we goes to New Orleans.

I satisfy then I lost my people and ain't never goin' to see them no more in this world, and I never did. They has three big trader yards in New Orleans, and I hear the traders say that town twenty-five mile square. I ain't like it so well, 'cause I ain't like it 'bout that big river. We hears some of 'em say there's gwine throw a long war, and us all think what they buys us for if we's gwine to be set free? Some was still buyin' niggers every fall, and us think it too funny they kept on fillin' up when they gwine be emptyin' out soon.

They have big sandbars and planks fix 'round the nigger yards, and they have watchmans to keep them from runnin' 'way in the swamp. Some of the niggers they have just picked up on the road, they steals them. They calls them "wagon boy" and "wagon gal." They has one big mulatto boy they stole 'long the road that way, and he massa find out 'bout him and come and git him and take him back. And a woman what was a seamster [seamstress], a man what knowed her seed her in the pen. He done told her massa, and he come right down and git her. She sho' was proud to git out. She was stole from 'long the road, too. You sees, if they could steal the niggers and sell 'em for the good money, them traders could make plenty money that way.

At last Colonel Fortescue, he buy me and kept me. He a

fighter in the Mexican War, and he come to New Orleans to buy slaves. He takes me up the Red River to Shreveport and then by the buggy to Liberty, in Texas.

The colonel, he a good massa to us. He 'lows us to work the patch of ground for ourselves, and maybe have a pig or a couple chickens for ourselves, and he allus make out to give us plenty to eat.

The massa, when a place fill up, he allus pick and move to a place where there ain't so much people. That how come the colonel first left Alabama and come to Texas, and to the place they calls Beef Head then, but calls Gran' Cane now.

When us come to Gran' Cane, a nigger boy git stuck on one us house girls, and he run away from he massa and follow us. It were a wooly country, and the boy outrun he chasers. I heared the dogs after him, and he torn and bleedin' with the brush. He run upstair in the gin house. The dogs set down by the door, and the dog-man, what hired to chase him, he drug him down and throw him in the horse hole [watering hole] and tells the two dogs to swim in and git him. They boy so scairt he yell and holler, but the dogs nip and pinch him good with they claws and teeth. When they lets the boy out the water hole, he all bit up. When he massa learn how mean the dog-men been to the boy, he 'fuses to pay the fee.

I gits married in slavery times to George Fortescue. The massa, he marry us sort of like the justice of the peace. But my husband, he git kilt in Liberty when he cuttin' down a tree and it fall on him. I ain't never marry no more.

I sho' was glad when Freedom come, 'cause they just ready to put my little three-year-old boy in the field. They took 'em young. I has another baby call Mittie, and she too young to work. I don't know how many chillen I's have, and sometimes I sits and tries to count 'em. They's seven livin', but I had 'bout fourteen.

They was pretty hard on the niggers. Iffen us have the baby us only 'lowed to stay in the house for one month to card and spin, and then us has to get out in the field. They allus blow the horn for us mammies to come up and nuss the babies.

I seed plenty sojers 'fore Freedom. They's the Democrats [Confederate soldiers], 'cause I never seed no Yankees. Us niggers used to wash and iron for them. At night us seed those sojers peepin' 'round the house, and us run 'way in the brush.

When Freedom come, us was layin' by the crop, and the massa, he give us a gen'rous part of that crop and us move. We gits on all right after Freedom, but it hard at first 'cause us didn't know how to do for ourselves. But we has to learn.

Sarah Ashley

A small, white-haired negress of quite ordinary manner, Sarah Ashley, ninety-three, tells a bitter story of her youth. At times her pronunciation is almost unintelligible as she recalls her experiences in a slave speculator's gang, her auction on the block in New Orleans, and strenuous days on a cotton plantation in Texas. Sarah's home at Goodrich, Texas, is comfortable—a clean-looking frame cottage surrounded by well-kept outbuildings, cultivated fields, and a liberal variety of chickens of many breeds, pecking busily around the doorstep.

I ain't able to do nuthin' no mo'. I's just plumb give out. I stay here all by myse'f. My daughter, Georgia Grime, she uster live with me, but she been dead fo' (four) year now. Since then, I been here all by myse'f. I try to git somebody to stay here with me but look like nobody wanter do that.

I was bo'n in Miss'ippi. I was 'bout five years old when I left there and come here. Mister Henry Thomas, he buys us and bring us here. He was a spec'lator. He buy up lots o' niggers and sell

Sarah Ashley

'em. Us fambly was separated. My udder two sisters and my fadder was sold to a man, I never know he name, in Alabama. I stay with the spec'lator's gang fo' five or ten year. Then they put me up on a block and bid me off. That was in N'Yawlins [New Orleans]. I was scared and cry, but they put me up there anyway. They sold me and my two sisters. They take me to Gregory. I think they pay 'bout a thousand dollar fo' me. Mister Thomas, he trabble [travel] 'roun' and buy and sell, buy and sell niggers. They didn't sell us fo' a long spell. Us stay in the spec'lator's drove.

After 'while, Mister Mose Davis from Cold Spring, Texas, buy us. He was buyin' up little chillen fo' he chillen. He bought me and a gal, and they buy a fambly from Georg'y [Georgia]. That was 'bout fo' year fo' [before] the first war. I was nineteen when the burst of freedom come in June, and I git turn loose.

I was workin' in the fiel' then. I uster work fo' a ol' lady, 73 year ol'. They uster have niggers to wait on the ol' people when they git disable. I uster hafter wait on her t'roo [through] the night. She was real sickly fo' three year. The ol' lady was like a mudder to me. That was ol' Mistus Betsy. Then they was Many Davis and Mose Davis, the marster and mistus. On the day they bury po' Miz Betsy, after the fun'ral Mister Mose, he come to me and say, "Pack up all yo' clothes, you comin' home to work in the fiel'." I work in the cotton fiel'. I sho' did hate it when that ol' lady die.

Little while after that, the ol' marster, he go off to buy mo' niggers. He go east. He was on a boat and git stove up, and he die and never come back no mo'. Us never see him no mo' after that trip. When the war bust out, he two sons fight in the battles.

I uster hafter pick cotton. Sometime I pick three hunnerd pound of cotton and tote it a mile to the cotton house. Some pick three hunnerd to eight hunnerd pounds of cotton and hafter tote the bag fo' a whole mile to the gin. Iffen they didn't do they work, they git whip 'til they have blister on 'em. Then iffen they didn't do it, a man on a hoss went down the rows and whip with a paddle made with holes in it and bust the blisters. I never git whip, 'cause I always git my three hunnerd pound. Us have to go in the fiel' so early, they blow the ho'n [horn] so early sometime they don't have time to cook fo' [before] daylight. Us hafter take us vittles to the fiel' in a bucket iffen we didn't have time to cook 'em.

Marster had a log house. 'Twarn't very nice. 'Twarn't no frame house. Slaves, they live in little houses. They quarters houses, they was strowed 'long in rows. The nigger quarters was fur from the big house as that house there.

There warn't no meetin's of no kin' 'lowed in the quarters. The bossman even whip them when they have prayer meetin'. Sometimes us run off at night to go to dances and camp meetin's, but I was plumb growed up 'fo' I ever went to chu'ch. I go to Sunday school with the white chillen to take care of 'em. They couldn't learnt me to sing no songs, 'cause I didn't have the spirit. I hear them sing, "Let the light shine." Nobudy can't sing when they ain't got the spirit to sing. I never learn to edication [education]. Books don't mean nuthin' to me, 'cept so much black and white.

The niggers 'roun' there never git 'nough to eat, so they kept stealin' stuff all the time. They give 'em a peck of meal to last a week. Just cornmeal, meat, sugar, and 'taters. Iffen you raise hawg the udder niggers steal 'em. They had a big box under the fireplace where they kept all the pig and chickens what they steal down in salt. Us hafter be keerful with how us eat, 'cause iffen some of the niggers find out 'bout it they run and tell the boss so he not make 'em work so hard. Iffen us find out what nigger do that to us, never have nuthin' to do with him no mo'.

When I was with the white lady, one time I seed a man in

the fiel' run 'way. The white men git the dogs out to hunt the nigger. They kotch him and put him in the front room. He so scare' he jump through the big winder [window] and break the glass all up. He jump out while us was eatin' breakfust. They sho' did whip him when they kotch him again.

The way they whip the niggers was to strip them off neckid and whip them 'til they make blisters and bust the blisters. Then they take salt and red pepper and put in the wounds. Aferward, they wash and grease them and put sumpthin' on to keep them from bleedin' to def' [death], but I never see them do it. I hear that sometime they put the nigger dawgs after them, and the dawgs kotch them and cat them up, but I never see nuthin' of that.

When the bossman tol' us Freedom was come, he didn't like it, but he give all of we'uns a bale of cotton and some corn what us could do what we wanter with. He ax [asked] us to stay and help with the crop, but we-uns was so glad to git 'way, nobody stay. I went to town and sol' mine. I git 'bout fifty dollars for it, and then I lent it to a nigger man what never pay me back to this day. That sho' the way of the wicked, 'cause here I's still livin', and he been dead since just a few year after Freedom come.

Then I got no place to go and no corn and cotton, so I go off to cook fo' a white man name Dick Cole. He s'posen [supposed] to gimme five dollar a month, or sixty dollar a year, but he never pay me no money. He wanter gimme it in clothes and eats, 'cause he has a little sto' [store].

I's gittin' so ol' I don't go to town or work out no mo'. Sometime at Chissmus [Christmas], I go up to Judge Murphy's fo' the big holiday dinner. I don't git no pension, 'cause I s'pose to have too much land. It ain't good fo' no woman to be 'lone like I is in this house.

Ben Simpson

Ben Simpson was ninety years old when he was interviewed. Born in Norcross, Georgia, he was taken to Austin, Texas. In Austin he was harshly treated and kept in chains by his master. He did not obtain his freedom until three years after the Civil War, when his master was hanged for horse stealing. After the war he wandered through the frontier until captured and taken to the estate of a General Houston (Sam Houston, governor of Texas and hero of the Texas Revolution died in 1863), where he was given a job and eventually married. Simpson's is a particularly brutal account, epitomizing the horror of the slavery system.

Sir, I was born in Norcross, Georgia, before they were any towns much in the state. I's ninety years old. My father's name was Roger Stielszen. My mother's name was Betty Stielszen. Master Earl Stielszen captured them in Africa and brought them to Georgia. My master, he then got killed, and I became his son's property, and he was a killer. He let me and sister belong to him. He sells my sister, because she was a big and healthy, good-lookin' Negro girl. He gets good price for her. She name Emma

Stielszen. After he comes to Texas, Boss, we never had no home, nor any quarters. When nighttime comes, he have chain that locks around our necks, then locks it around a tree. Boss, our bed were the ground. Master, he get into trouble there in Georgia. See, he get branding arn [iron], brand seven men. My mother and myself, then sister Emma. Boss, that nearly kilt my mother. He brand her in breast, then on the back between the shoulders. Boss, he brand all us men that way, 'cause he was a mean man. My mother was all the Negro women he have until sister Emma get big enough to take care all them Negro men, 'cause she was the wife of all seven Negro slaves.

But what I's fixin' to tell you was when he gets into trouble there in Georgia. He got him two good stropping horses and has him covered wagon. Then he chains all the slaves he have around the necks and fastens to the horses and makes all the slaves walk the same way, 'cept sister Emma, and she had to walk some time. All she get to ride was the couplin' pole that come out behind the wagon bed about three feet. Somewhere on the road, it went to snowing, and master would not let us have shoes or anything to wrap around our feet. Then we had to sleep on the ground in all that snow. Boss, he had a great long whip platted out of rawhide, and when one of the Negro begins to fall behind or give out, he would hit him with that whip. And he would take all the hide ever' time master hit a Negro. Mother, she give out on the way somewhere about the line of Texas. Her feet got raw and bleeding, and her legs swell plum out of shape. Then master, he just take out his gun and shot her. While she was dying, he kick her two or three times and say damn a Negro that couldn't stand anything. He didn't need them anyway, 'cause he could get plenty more. Wouldn't bury mother, just left her laying where he shot her at.

He come plum to Austin, Texas, through that snow. Boss,

you know that time they wasn't any law against killing Negro slaves. After he got to Austin, he take up farming and changes his name to Alex Simpson. Then, Boss, he changes our name on that there plantation. He cuts logs and builds his home on the side of one of them mountains. Then at night, he stakes us out under one of them cedar trees, and all he feeds us was raw meat, green corn. Sometimes he put it in the ashes and burn it. Boss, I's eat a many green weed, 'cause I would get hungry. Master would work us all day without stopping. He never let us eat at dinnertime.

Master, he sold sister Emma when she was about 15 years old, just before her baby was born. I's never seen her since, 'cause the people took her north. After master come to Texas, he never did get us any clothes. We went naked—that was the way he worked us. Captain Master was an outlaw. He come to Texas and dealt in stolen horses. And just before he was hung for stealing horses, he married a young Spanish girl. He sure was mean to her, whipped her because she wanted him to live right and treat his slaves right. Yes, sir, bless her heart. She was the best girl in the world. She was the best thing God ever put life in the world. She would cry and cry ever' time master would go off. She would let us alone and feed us good. Mistress Selena, [one time] she turn us loose and let us go. [We] wash in the creek there close by, and she had just unfastened the chain around our necks and give us great big pot of cooked meat and cornbread, and up he rides. Just gets his horses, never says word but come to see what we eatin', then pick up his whip and whipped her until she fall. If I could have got loose, I would have killed him. Then I swore if I ever got loose, I would overpower him and kill him. But it wasn't long after that he failed to come home, and some people found him hanging to a tree. Boss, that was after the war long time, when he got hung

I don't remember much about the war, except what mistress

told us. Master, he married her during the war. He hide out and wouldn't go to the war. Said when the war closed, he would be rich man, 'cause he was stealing all the time. Mistress told us one day that we was supposed to be free, but master didn't turn us loose. Then one night about three years after the war, he stole a bunch of horses, and some white men caught him, and they hung him to a limb. Then mistress liberated us, but she make us go and take him down from the tree limb and buried him. But, Boss, that white man was so mean he couldn't be still after he was dead, 'cause he would wiggle around every time one us slave touch him. I's afraid that man going to come to life and kill him a bunch of slaves.

They was a hundred or more acres in the farm. Then he have a hole in the mountainside where he kept his stock. No, sir, never seen any slaves sold except Sister Emma. The man just ask master what he take for her, and master told him, so they traded. Boss, I cried a week, 'cause she was the only kin that I knew anything about. I didn't know who father's people was.

I never saw slaves in chains, except the seven that master owned. We wore chains all the time. Was never took off when we was at work. We either drug the chains or was snapped together, and at night we were locked to a tree to keep us from trying to run off. He didn't have to do that, 'cause we were afraid to run. We knew master would kill us. Besides, he had already branded us, and they was no way to get that off.

We only had Sunday to rest. He would work us on Saturday. When we got sick, we had to be pretty sick. If we wasn't, master worked us just the same. If we were too sick to go, master left us locked to a tree. He never get a doctor or give us anything to take. Said we wasn't worth the trouble.

The first year after the war that I was free, I's had a hard time getting something to eat. All I had to eat was what I could find and steal, because I was afraid to ask for work. I just went wild and went to the woods, but, thank God, a bunch of men took their dogs and run me down. They carried me to their place with General Houston, who had some Negroes on his place, and made these Negroes feed me and keep me with them until I's got well and able to work. Then he [Houston] give me a job, and I's married one his Negro girls—Emma Brown—before I's leave them. We just have home wedding, and they had big supper and dance for a week. Yes, sir, Boss, I's plum out of place there at my own weddin', 'cause it wasn't a year before that I's a wild Negro. We have thirteen children—seven girls and six boys. I dunno how many grandchildren or great-grandchildren I have. There are so many I can't count them.

I didn't know too much about what the war was fought for, except I thought maybe the government would give us Negroes a good job and some spending money. I's farmed ever since I was freed, 'cause that was all I could do, as I didn't have education or know anything else to do. I's generally made lots of cotton, until those last few years. I's gotten too old to farm or do any kind of work. All the childrens are married and gone. I thinks since the war was fought and freed the Negro that it has been a great period for the Negro race, as they have become educated and can hold 'most any kind of job. Some is government men and can hold office. Yes, sir, Boss, I's seen the KKK, but they never did get after this old Negro, 'cause when I's gets free I tend to me own business. I never did vote, 'cause I's couldn't read and write. But I's do think the younger Negroes ought to be allowed to vote more'n they do, 'cause they have to shoulder the same load that the white man has today. This old Negro is getting small pension from the government. 'Course I's not got much longer to stay here, but I's done got ready to see God when I's die. But, Boss, I hopes my old master is not up there to torment this old Negro again.

Anderson and Minerva Edwards

━━

Anderson and Minerva Edwards, a Negro Baptist preacher and his
wife, were both slaves on joining plantations in Rusk County, near
Henderson. Anderson was born on March 12, 1844, as a slave of
Major Matt Gaud, and Minerva was born February 2, 1850, as a
slave of Major Flannigan. In this way, Anderson and Minerva met
before Emancipation. They continued to work for their respective
masters until about three years after the war, when they moved to
Harrison County with their parents. Later they married and reared
a family of sixteen children. Six of their boys are still living and
employed on public works in Marshall. Anderson and Minerva live
in a small, but comfortable, farmhouse, two miles north of Marshall
on Macedonia Road. They draw a fourteen-dollar-per-month
pension from the government.

━━

[*Anderson begins the narrative.*]

My father was Sandy Flannigan. He run off from his first
master on the eastern shore of Maryland and come to Texas. Here,
he was picked up by a slave buyer who sold chances on him. If
they could find his master in Maryland, he would have to go back

Anderson and Minerva Edwards

to him. If they couldn't find who he belonged to, the chances was good. Wash Edwards, of Panola County, bought the chance on Pappy, but he run off from him, too, and come to Major Flannigan's in Rusk County. Finally, Major Flannigan had to pay four thousand dollars in all to get a clear title to him. I hear him say that he come to Marshall before there was anything here, and how he used to catch squirrels and rabbits where the square is now.

My mother was named Minerva and belonged to Major Gaud. I was born there on his plantation on March 12, 1844. You can ask the tax man at Marshall 'bout my age. He's fix my 'semption [exemption] papers since I was sixty. I had seven brothers and two sisters. They was Frank, Joe, Sandy, Gene, Preston, William, Sarah, and Delilah. They all lived to be old folks. The baby chile just die last year. Folks was more healthy when I was growing up than now. They didn't die young, like folks do now. I's ninety-three now and ain't dead. 'Fact, I feels right pert most of the time.

My mistress was named Mary. She and Master Matt had three boys and one girl. They lived in a hewed log house that is still standing now, there near Henderson. The quarters were across the road from master's house and set all in a row. He owned three families of slaves. Master had lots of horses, sheep, and cows. Pappy was herder for him 'til he was freed. The government run a big tan-yard [the section or portion of a tannery housing tanning vats] there on Major Gaud's place. One of my uncles was shoemaker for the government. Just 'bout the time of the war, I was piddling 'round the tannery and a government man say to me, "Boy, I'll give you a thousand dollars to go get me a drink of water." And he did, but it was 'fedate [Confederate] money that got killed, so it done me no good. Mammy was a weaver and made all our clothes. Master give us plenty to eat and wear. Fact is, he treated us kinda like his own boys. 'Course he would whip us when we needed it, but not like I seed darkies whipped on other farms. He give us a pass most any time we wanted it, when we wanted to go anywhere, so we wouldn't get hurt by them patterollers. The other niggers call Major Gaud's slaves free niggers. We could hear them crying and moaning on 'joining farms when they was putting it on them. If they would have gone on and took it right when they correct them, it would have lightened the burden. Some of the niggers just naturally had hard heads and would run off when they whip them. That just made it harder on them.

I worked in the field from one year's end to the other. When we come in at dusk, we had to cook and eat supper and be in bed by nine o'clock. We slept on bunks that had straw and shuck mattresses. All the cooking was done on the fireplace. Master would give us most anything he had to eat 'cept biscuits. Dat ashcake warn't bad eating. It was cooked by putting cornmeal batter in shucks and baking it in the ashes. We didn't work in the field on Sunday but had so many stock to tend that it kept us busy Sunday same as Monday. Master Gaud was a wicked man and didn't care anything about God, heaven, and his outfit. If we went to church, it was mistress that took us. She was a religious woman and allus went to church on Sunday. The first church I went to was under a big mulberry tree there on the place. A white man done the preaching. Master had told us that if we be good niggers and obey him that we would go to heaven. But I felt all the time that there was something better than that for me. So I kept praying for it 'til I felt the change in my heart. I was by myself down by a spring when I found the Lord.

When the darkies prayed in slavery, they darsn't let the white folks know 'bout it, or they beat them to death. When we prayed, we turned a wash pot down to the ground to catch the voice. We prayed lots in slavery to be free, and the Lord heard our prayer. We didn't have no songbooks. The Lord give us our songs. When we sing them at night 'round the fireplace, it would be just whispering-like, so the white folks not hear us. We would hum them as we worked in the field. One of our favorite songs went like this:

> My kneebones am aching.
> My body's racking with pain.
> I really believe I's a chile of God.
> This ain't my home, 'cause heaven's my aim.

Master Gaud used to give big corn shuckings and cotton pickings. The women cooked up big dinners, and master would give us whiskey. We've shucked corn all night lots of times. On Saturday nights, they made us sing and dance. We made our own instruments, which was gourd fiddles and quill flutes. Generally, Christmas was just like any other day, but I got Santa Claus twice during slavery. Master give me a sack of molasses candy and some biscuits. That was whole lots to me.

They never 'lowed a nigger to have a book. If we did learn to write, and they knowed it, they'd cut our fingers off. When a slave died, they made the box there on the place, and the folks go to the burying. But there warn't no crying, singing, or praying 'lowed.

The Vinsons and the Frys, that lived 'joining farms to Master Gaud, sold slaves. I's seed niggers sold and chained together like stock and drive' off in herds by a white man on a horse. They'd sell babies away from their mothers. The Lord never did intend such as that.

I believe in that ghost and haunt business yet. I seen one when I was a boy. It was right after Mammy died. Me and Pappy and the other chil'ren lived there in one of Major Gaud's cabins. I had gone to bed and woke up and saw it come in the door. It had a body, legs, and tail like a wooly poodley dog, and a face like a man. He walked over to the fireplace and raised the lid off the skillet of potatoes setting on the hearth. Then he walked over to my bed, raised up the cover, and crawled in bed. I hollered so loud it woke all the niggers on the place. Pappy say what's the matter with me? I tell him I seed a ghost. He says I was crazy, but I guess I knows a haunt when I sees one.

And that ain't the only haunt I's seen. Minerva there can tell you 'bout that haunted house we lived in near Marshall, just after we was married.

[*Minerva, sitting nearby, said, "'Deed I can," and proceeded to relate the following account.*]

The next year after me and Anderson was married we moved on a place northwest of Marshall. It once belonged to some white folks. The man was real mean to his wife and would beat her up and choke her nearly to death. Finally she died there in the house, and he left the country. Anderson rented the place, and we moved in. I didn't believe in haunts then, but I do now. One night we saw that woman that died come all 'round the house with a light in her hand. When she comes in the house, it would light up all over. Neighbors said it look like it was on fire. One night she came and walked 'round the house with a black hearse following her. We left our crop and moved away from there and ain't gone back yit to gather our crop. 'Fore we moved in, the place had been vacant since the woman died there. One night Charlie Williams that lives in Marshall and runs a store out by the T&P Hospital got drunk and went out there to sleep. While he was sleeping that woman come on him and nearly choked him to death.

Ain't nobody lived in that house since we was there. The niggers all tell us they don't see how we lived there long as we did.

[*Anderson resumes his story.*]

I 'member when the war started. Master's boy, George Gaud, saddled up old Bob, his pony, and left for the war. He stayed six months before he come back home. When he rode up master say, "How's the war, George?" Master George say, "It's hell. Me and Bob has been running Yankees ever since we left." 'Fore the war, master didn't ever say much about slavery, but when he heard the slaves was freed, he cursed and say, "God never did intend to free niggers." And he cussed 'til he died. They didn't tell us we was free 'til a year after the war. One day a bunch of Yankee soldiers rode up to the place. Master and mistress saw them coming and hid out. They walked into the house. Mammy was churning, and one of them kicked the churn over and say, "Get out, you's just as free as I is." Then they ransacked the place and broke out all the window lights. When they left, it look like a storm had hit the house. Master come back to the house, and that's when he started on a cussing spree that lasted as long as he lived.

'Bout four years after the war, Pappy come and took me to Harrison County, and I's lived here ever since. Minerva's Pappy moved from the Flannigan place to a 'joining farm 'bout the same time, and several years later we was married. We married at her house. She wore a blue serge [a durable twill fabric] suit, and I wore a cutaway Prince Albert suit. There was 'bout two hundred folks at the wedding. The next day they give us an infair [affair] and a big dinner. We raised sixteen children to be grown. Six of the boys are still living and working in Marshall.

I's been preaching the gospel and farming since slavery time. I joined the chu'ch eighty-three years ago, when I was a slave of

Master Gaud. They took me in to the white chu'ch and baptized me down there in the spring branch close to where I found the Lord. I started preaching right after I joined the chu'ch. 'Course when I started preaching, I was a slave and couldn't read or write. 'Til Freedom, I had to preach what they told me to. Master made me preach to the other niggers that the Good Book say that if niggers obey their master they would go to heaven. I knew there was something better for them, but I darsn't tell them, lest I done it on the sly. That I did lots. I told niggers, but not so master could hear it, if they keep praying, that the Lord would hear their prayers and set them free. I's preached most all over Panola and Harrison Counties. I started the Edward's Chapel there in Marshall and pastored it until a few years ago. It's named for me. I don't preach much now, 'cause I can't hold out to walk that far, and I got no way to go.

Josephine Howard

━━

*Josephine Howard was born in slavery on the Walton plantation
near Tuscaloosa, Alabama. She does not know her age, but when Mr.
Walton moved to Texas before the Civil War, she was old enough to
work in the fields. Josephine is blind and very feeble. She lives with
a daughter at 1520 Arthur Street, Houston, Texas.*

━━

Lord have mercy, I been here a thousand year, seems like.
'Course I ain't been here so long, but it seems like it when I gets
to thinkin' back. It was a long time since I was born, long 'fore
the war. Mammy's name was Leonora, and she was cook for Marse
Tim Walton, what had the plantation at Tuscaloosa. That am in
Alabamy. Papa's name was Joe Tatum, and he lived on the place
'joinin' ourn. 'Course, Papa and Mammy wasn't married like
folks now, 'cause them times the white folks just put slave men
and women together like hosses or cattle.

They always done tell us it am wrong to lie and steal, but
why did the white folks steal my mammy and her mammy? They
lives close to some water somewheres over in Africy, and the

━━ 49

men come in a little boat to the sho' and tell them he got presents on the big boat. Most the men am out huntin', and my mammy and her mammy gets took out to that big boat. They locks them in a black hole, what Mammy say so black you can't see nothin'. That the sinfullest stealin' they is.

The captain keep them locked in that black hole 'til that boat gets to Mobile, and they is put on the block and sold. Mammy is 'bout twelve year old, and they am sold to Marse Tim. Grandma dies in a month, and they puts her in the slave graveyard.

Mammy am a nurse gal 'til she get older, and then cook. Then old Marse Tim puts her and Papa together, and she has eight chillen. I reckon Marse Tim warn't no worser than other white folks. The nigger driver sho' whip us, with the reason and without the reason. You never knowed. If they done took the notion, they just lays it on you, and you can't do nothin'.

One mornin', we is all herded up. Mammy am cryin' and say they goin' to Texas but can't take Papa. He don't belong to them. That the lastest time we ever seed Papa. Us and the women am put in wagons, but the men slaves am chained together and has to walk.

Marse Tim done get a big farm up by Marshall but only live a year there. His boys run the place. They just like they papa, work us and work us. Lord have mercy, I hear that call in the mornin' just like it was yesterday. "All right, everybody out, and you better get out iffen you don't want to feel that bullwhip 'cross you back."

My gal I lives with don't like me to talk 'bout them times. She say it ain't no more, and it ain't good to think 'bout it. But when you has lived in slave times, you ain't goin' to forget them, no, sir! I's old and blind and no 'count, but I's alive. In slave times, I'd be dead long time ago, 'cause white folks didn't have no use for old niggers and get shed of them one way or the other.

It ain't 'til the sojers come we is free. They [the Walton family] wants us to get in the pickin', so my folks and some more stays. They didn't know no place to go to. Mammy done took sick and die, and I hires out to cook for Missy Howard and marries her coachman, what am Woodson Howard. We farms and comes to Houston nigh sixty year ago. They has mule cars then. Woodson gets a job drivin', and 'fore he dies we raise three boys and seven gals, but all 'cept two gals am dead now. They takes care of me, and that all I know 'bout myself.

Sam Jones Washington

Sam Jones Washington, age eighty-eight, was born a slave of Sam Young, who owned a ranch along the Colorado River in Wharton County, Texas. Sam was trained to be a cowhand and worked for his master until 1868, receiving wages after he was freed. He farmed until 1905, then moved to Fort Worth and worked in the packing plants until 1931. He lives at 3520 Columbus Avenue, Fort Worth, and is supported by an eleven-dollar-per-month old-age pension, supplemented by what he raises in his garden and makes out of a few hogs.

How old I is? I's sixteen year when Surrender come. I knows that, 'cause of massa's statement. All us niggers gits the statement when Surrender comes. I's seed plenty slave days.

Massa Young run a small farm 'long the Colorado River, and him own many slaves. There my mammy and her six chillen, and Jamoria and her four chillens. My pappy am not on the place. I don't know my pappy. Him am what they calls the travelin' nigger. They have him come for service, and when they gits what they

Sam Jones Washington

wants, he go back to he massa. The womens on Massa Young place not married.

Massa raise just a little cotton, that two womens and the chillen could tend to, and some veg'tables and such. Us have lots of good food. Us sleep in the sleepin' room next to massa's house, but I sleeps in Massa's room.

One night Massa say, "Don't tie my hoss to the stake tonight." But I's sleepy and gits the nodfies and drops off to sleep. Mammy shake me and say, "Did you stake the hoss?" Massa sees that hoss in the mornin' and say, "You done stake that hoss, and I told you not to." He gives me a couple licks, and I learns to do what I's told. He never whip nobody, not the hard whippin' like other niggers git. He am a good massa.

I first run errand, and then Massa learns me to ride so's I could sit the hoss. Then I stays out with the cattle most the time, and I's tickled. I sho' likes to ride and rope them cattle, and Massa allus fix me up with good clothes, and good hoss, and good saddle. I stays there 'til long after Surrender.

Us have stampedes from the cattle. That am cust'mary with them critters. That mean, ride the hoss to turn the cattle. Us ride to side the leader and crowd him and force him to turn, and keep forcin' him, and by and by them critters am runnin' in the circle. That keep them from scatterment. That sho' dangerous ridin'. If the hoss throw you off, them cattle stamp you to death. Gabriel sho' blow he horn for you then!

I sho' 'joys [enjoys] that business, 'cause we'uns have the good time. Us go to town and have fun. One time I comes near gittin' in trouble, but it ain't my fault. I's in town, and Massa, too, and a white man come to me, and him sho' the drink. "Who you 'long to, nigger?" he say. "I's Massa Young's nigger," I says polite-like. "You looks like the smart nigger, and I's the notion to smack you one," he say. "You better not smack me any," I says. You understand, that the way Massa raise me. I don't understand some cruel white mens gits the arg'ments, just for the chance to shoot the nigger. Massa am standin' nearby, and him come up and say, "If you touches that nigger, I'll put the bullet through you." That man see Massa have no foolishment in he words and gits gwine. But if Massa not there, Gabriel blow the horn for this nigger's Jubilee, right then, yes, sir.

I comes near gittin' cotched by the patterollers once. I just twelve then and 'nother nigger and me, us want some cane stalk. It good to eat raw, you knows. Just peel the bark off and chew that inside. Well, we'uns in the man's cane patch, breakin' them stalks, and they makes the poppin' noise. A patteroller come by and hear that poppin' and holler, "Who's there in the cane patch?" Us didn't answer him, no, sir. I 'cides right quick that I don't like cane, and I comes 'way from that patch. I outsmarts and outruns that patteroller. I keeps to the cane fields and the woods, and I runs this way and that way. I twists 'round, so he couldn't follow my tracks. Like the snake's track, you can't tell if it am gwine north or comin' back, Lawd almighty! How fast I runs! I stays 'head of my shadow, I tells you, I's a-gwine!

The war? White man, we'uns didn't know there am the war. We seed some sojers at the start, but that all. One day Massa say to me, "After this, you gits fifteen dollars the month wages." I works for him three more years, and then he sold out. Then I goes farmin' 'til 1905. I works in the packin' plants here in Fort Worth then, 'til I's wore out, 'bout six year ago. Now I raises the hogs, not very many, and does what work I can git. That pension from the state sho' helps me. With that, and the hogs, and the little garden I gits by, and so I lives.

Was I every married? Man, man, three times. First time, 'bout 1869, and we'uns gits the seperment [separation] in 1871. That woman sho' deal me mis'ry! She am the troublin' woman. Then 'bout 1873, I marries 'gain, and she die 'fore long. Then in 1905, I marries 'gain, and she's dead, too. I never has the chillen. I's just 'lone and old now, and stay here 'til my time comes. I 'spect it quite a spell yet, 'cause I's got lots of substance left, yes, sir.

Rosina Howard

Rosina Howard does not know just where she was born. The first
thing she remembers is that she and her parents were purchased
by Colonel Pratt Washington, who owned a plantation near
Garfield, in Travis County, Texas. Rosina, who is a very pleasant
and sincere person, says she has had a tough life since she was
free. She receives a monthly pension of fourteen dollars, for which
she expresses gratitude. Her address is 1201 Chestnut Street,
Austin, Texas.

+===+===+===+===+===+===+===+===+===+===+===+===+===+===+===+===+===+

When I's a gal, I's Rosina Slaughter, but folks call me Zina.
Yes, sir, it am Zina that, and Zina this. I says I's born April 9,
1859, but I 'lieve I's elder. It was somewhere in Williamson
County, but I don't know the massa's name. My mammy was
Lusanne Slaughter, and she was stout, but in her last days she got
to be a li'l bit of a woman. She died only last spring, and she was
a hundred eleven years old.

Papa was a Baptist preacher to the day of he death. He had
asthma all his days. I 'member how he had the sorrel hoss and

would ride off and preach under some arbor bush. I rid with him on he hoss.

First thing I 'member is us was bought by Massa Colonel Pratt Washington from Massa Lank Miner. Massa Washington was purty good man. He boys, George and John Henry, was the only overseers. Them boys treat us nice. Massa always ride up he hoss after dinnertime. He hoss was a bay call Sank. The fields was in the bottom of the Colorado River. The big house was on the hill, and us could see him comin'. He weared a tall, beaver hat.

The reason allus watch for him am that he boy, George, try learn us our ABCs in the field. The workers watch for massa, and when they seed him a-ridin' down the hill, they starts singin' out, "Ole hawg 'round the bench. Ole hawg 'round the bench."

That the signal, and then everybody starts workin' like they have something after them. But I's too young to learn much in the field, and I can't read today and have to make the cross when I signs for my name.

Each chile have he own weed tray. There was old Aunt, and she done all the cookin' for the chillen in the depot. That what they calls the place all the chillen stays 'til their mammies come home from the field. Aunt Alice have the big pot to cook in, out in the yard. Some days we had beans and some day peas. She put great hunks of salt bacon in the pot and bake plenty cornbread, and give us plenty milk.

Some big chillen have to pick cotton. Old Junus was the cullud overseer for the chillen, and he sure mean to them. He carry a stick and use it, too.

One day the blue-bellies come to the fields. They Yankee sojers, and they tell the slaves they free. Some stayed and some left. Papa took us and move to the Craft plantation, not far 'way, and farm there.

I been married three time. First to Peter Collinsworth. I

quit him. Second to George Heard. We stayed together 'til he die, and have five chillen. Then I marries he brother, Jim Heard. [Editor's note: The interviewer apparently recorded the names of two of Rosina's husbands as "Heard," when their name was actually "Howard." This mistake probably came about because the interviewer was transcribing the name phonetically.] I tells you the truth, Jim never did work much. He'd go fishin' and chop weed by the days, but not many days. He suffered with the piles. I done the housework and look after the chillen, and then go out and pick two hundred pound cotton a day. I was a cripples, since one of my boys birthed. I git the rheumatis', and my knees hurt so much sometime I rub wet sand and mud on them to ease the pain.

We had a house at Barton Springs with two rooms, one log and one box. I never did like it up there, and I told Jim I's gwine. I did, but he come and get me.

Since Freedom, I's been through the toughs. I had to do the man's work, chop down trees, and plow the fields, and pick cotton. I want to tell you how glad I is to git my pension. It sure is nice of the folks to take care of me in my old age. Befo' I got the pension, I had a hard time. You can sho' say I's been through the toughs.

Gus Johnson

*Gus Johnson, age ninety or more, was born a slave of Mrs. Betty
Glover in Marengo County, Alabama. Most of his memories are of
his later boyhood in Sunnyside, Texas. He lives in an unkempt, little
lean-to house in the north end of Beaumont, Texas. There is no
furniture but a broken-down bed and an equally dilapidated trunk
and stove. Gus spends most of his time in the yard, working in his
vegetable garden.*

They brung thirty-six of us here in a boxcar from Alabama.
Yes, sir, that's where I come from—Marengo County. Us belong
to old Missy Betty Glover. My daddy name August Glover and
my mammy Lucinda. Old Missy, she sho' treat us good, and I never
git whipped for anything 'cept lyin'. Old Missy, she do the whippin'.

Old Missy, she sho's a good woman, and all her white folks,
they used to go to church at White Chapel at 'leven in the
mornin'. Us cullud folks goes in the evenin'. Us never do no
work on Sunday, and on Saturday after twelve o'clock us can go
fishin' or huntin'.

They give the rations on Saturday, and that's 'bout five pound salt bacon, and a peck of meal, and some sorghum syrup. They make that syrup on the plantation. They's ten or twelve big clay kettles in a row, set in the furnace.

We have lots to eat, and if the rations run short we goes huntin' or fishin'. Some old men kills rattlesnakes and cook 'em like fish, and say they fish. I eat that many a time and never knowed it. 'Twas good, too.

They used to have a big house where they kept the chillen, 'cause the wolves and panthers was bad. Some mammies what suckle the chillen takes care of all the chillen durin' the daytime, and at night they own mammies come in from the field and takes them. Sometime Old Missy, she help nuss, and all the li'l niggers well cared for. When they gits sick, they makes the med'cine of herbs and well 'em that way.

When us left Alabama, us come through Meridian to Houston, and then to Hockley, and then to Sunnyside, 'bout 18 miles west of Houston. That a country with a lot of woods, and us set in to clean up the ground and clean up 150 acres to farm on. There're 'bout forty-seven hands, and more 'cumulates [accumulates]. They go back to Meridian for more, and brung 'em in a ox cart.

My brother, Bonsane Johnson, was one they brung on that trip. I had 'nother brother, Keen, what die when he 102 year old. Us was all long-life people, 'cause I have a gran' uncle what die when he was 135 year old. He and my grandma and grandpa come from South Caroline, and they was all Africa people. I heard them tell how they brung from Africa in the ship. My daddy he die at ninety-nine, and 'nother brother at 104.

Us see lots of sojers when us come through Meridian, and they the cavalry. They come ridin' up with high hats like beavers on they head, and us 'fraid of 'em, 'cause they told us they gwine take us to Cuba and sell us there.

When us first git to Texas it was cold—not sort a cold, but I mean cold. I shovel the snow many a day. They have the big common house. The white folks live upstairs, and the niggers sleep on the first floor. That to 'tect the white folks at night, but us have our own house for to lives in in the daytime, builded out of logs and daubed with mud and boards over that mud. They make the chimney out of sticks and mud, too, but us have no windows. In summer, us kind of live out in the brush arbor, what was cool.

Us have all kind of crops, and more'n a hundred acres in fruit, 'cause they brung all kind of trees and seed from Alabama. They was underground springs, and the water was sho' good to drink, 'cause in Mobile the water wasn't fitten to drink. It taste like it have the lump of salt melted in it. Us keep the butter and milk in the springhouse in them days, 'cause us ain't have no ice in them time.

Old Massa, he name Aden, and he brother name John, and they was way up yonder tall people. Old Massa die soon, and us have Missy to say what we do. All her overseers have to be good. She punish the slaves iffen they bad, but not whip 'em. She have the jail builded underground like the storm cave, and it have a drop door with a weight on it, so they couldn't git up from the bottom. It sho' was dark in that place.

In slavery time, us better be in by eight o'clock, better be in that house, better stick to the rule. I 'member after Freedom, Missy have the big celebration on Juneteenth [a celebration of the ending of slavery in Texas. It commemorates the date of June 19, 1865, when Union soldiers arrived in Galveston, Texas, with the news that the war had ended, and the slaves were free. The event is still widely celebrated in Texas and throughout the United States.] every year.

When war come to Texas, every plantation was conscrip' for the war, and my daddy was 'pointed [appointed] to select the able-body men off us place for to be sojers. My brother Keen was one of them. He come back all right, though.

When Freedom come, Missy give all the men niggers five hundred dollars each, but that 'federate [Confederate] money and have pictures of hosses on it. That the onliest money Missy have then. Old Missy Betty, she die in Sunnyside, Texas, when she 115 year old.

When I's eighteen year old, I marry a gal by the name Lucy Johnson. She dead now long ago. I got five livin' chillen somewhere, but I done lost track of 'em. One of them boys serve in the last war.

I been here thirty-six year, and I work most the time as house mover, what I work at twenty-six year. I'll be honest with you, I don't know how old I is, but it must be plenty, 'cause I 'member lots 'bout the war. I didn't see no fightin', but I knowed what as goin' on then.

Julia Frances Daniels

Julia Frances Daniels, born in 1848 somewhere in Georgia, lives with her daughter at 2523 Spring Street, Dallas, Texas. She is the mother of seventeen children and has no account of her grandchildren, but knows some of her great-grandchildren. She is of robust appearance. She is known at the church and in the neighborhood as Mother Daniels. She has recently started to learn reading and writing.

They's lots I disremembers, and they's lots I remembers. I remembers very well the year the war was over and the fighting all done with, 'cause that was the year I learned to plow, and that was the time I got married. That was the very year they learned me to plow. I learnt alright 'cause I warn't one slow to learn anything. Afore to that time, they ain't never had no hoe in the field for me at all. I just toted water most of the time for the ones in the field.

I never hardly had nothing to do when I lived with Old Man Denman. He was the one that owned my mother and father and

Julia Frances Daniels

all of us, until he 'vided some of us with Miss Lizzie, and she married Mr. Cramer. I just played around and picked up chunkwood and gathered hay for the beds and pulled shucks offen the burr-ends to make matresses. I was a skittish little youngun, and me and my sisters and brothers liked to play around in the woods by the spring.

I had plenty brothers and sisters. I remembers Tom, Harrison, George, Martha, Emmaline, Mandy, Elissa, Sophia, Savannah, and Neeley. They was all named Denman, 'cause my mother and father was Lottie and Boyd Denman, and they came from Georgia to Cherokee County, and then to Houston County near by to Crockett with Old Man Denman.

My father worked in the fields with Uncle Lot, and Dan, and Corry, and Sam, and my brothers, and some of the womens, and Uncle Joe. Uncle Joe, he was the driver. He is the one who is 'sponsible to get us up. He gits up afore day for the workin'. He whups us chilluns when we disbehaves.

But Briscoe is the overseer. We used to call him Old Briscoe. He is a white man. He can't never whup the grown mens like he is 'spose to 'cause they don't let him unless he goes to Old Man Denman, and I believe he is 'shamed to go very much. I seen them whup them though. Briscoe make them take off their shirt, and he whups them with a strap. Sometimes they have to buckle them to the ground. They don't like to get whuppin's, but they don't stay mad very long.

Now my mother was the cook in the Denman house, and she cooked for the Denmans, and our fambly, and Uncle Joe's fambly. She didn't have much time for anything but cookin' all the time. But she was the bestest cook. We had fine green gardens, and fine hogs, and beef. We used to eat collard greens and pork. We eat the pork until we got skittish of it. When they quit the pork and killed the beefs, they was just pourin' water on our wheel 'cause we liked best of anything the beef, and I do to this day, only I can't never get it.

Mr. Denman had a boy that killed squirrels and throwed them in the kitchen. The white folks eat them. You ain't never seen no white folks then that would eat rabbit. But I had a brother who hunted every time he gits the chance—mostly on Sundays. He would leave for the swamps before daybreak, and we would know when we hear him callin', "Oooooo, oooo-dah-dah-dah-ske-e-e-e-t-t-t-ttt," that he had sumpin'. That was just a make-up of his own, but we knowed they was rabbits for the pot.

All the mens don't hunt on Sundays, 'cause Uncle Joe used to hold meetin' out in front of his house on Sundays, and lots of other times, too. When we looked out the door, and seen Uncle Joe settin' the benches straight, and settin' his table out under the trees, and sweepin' clean the leaves, then we used to say: "Going to be meetin'." Sometime my mother don't hardly have no time to wash us to go, but sometimes she let us go and everything was so sweet and fine and lovely. They was the loveliest days that ever they was. Nighttimes, too, they'd make it between them, whether it would be at our house or Uncle Joe's. Uncle Joe was the only one could do any preachin'. We'd ask the niggers from other farms to come to the meetin's, and I used to say: "I likes a meetin' just as good as I likes a party." We used to sing:

Children of the Heavenly King,
As we join and let us sing.
Sing our Savior, worthy of praise.
Glory in His work and ways.
We are traveling home to God
In the way our fathers trod.
Christ our advocate is made.

When the crops is laid by is when we have the most parties. We used to dance, and sing, and have play-games. The reels was what I used to like, but I done quit that foolishness many years ago. I used to cut a step or two. I remembers a reel called the Devil's Dream. It was a fast song.

> Oh! the devil dreamt a dream.
> He dreamt it on a Friday.
> He dreamt he caught a sinner—

Then somebody would call out real loud:

> Oh! the devil, he dreamt a dream!

Old Man Denman was a great one for 'viding his property. When Miss Lizzie marries with Mr. Creame Cramer, which is her dead sister's husband, Old Man Denman gives me and two of my sisters to Miss Lizzie and to the Cramer place. We lived in the backyard in a little room by the back door.

Everything is fine and nice there, until one day Miss Lizzie says to me, "Julia, go down to the well and bring me some water." I go down to the well, and I see in the road a heap of men all in gray and ridin' horses coming our way. I runs back to the house and I'm a-calling Miss Lizzie. She says, "Where is my water?" I say, "Miss Lizzie, I's a-scared." She says, "What are you a-scared for?" I tell her about the mens, and she says, "Go on back and get the water, Julia. They ain't going to hurt you none. They just wants some water." I went back to the well, and I heard them make talk about a fight. Then I went back to the house, and some of the mens come up to the gate. They say to Mr. Cramer, "How're you, Creame?" And Mr. Cramer says, "I'm alright in my health, but I ain't so good in mind." They say, "What is the matter, Creame?"

And he says, "I want to be in the fight so bad."

When the mens were gone, I axed Miss Lizzie, "What they fightin' about?" She says, "They is fightin' about money." I say, "Where is they fightin'?" She says, "Over yonders somewheres." And that is all I know.

Right after that, Mr. Cramer went away, and we don't never see him no more. The word comes back from the fightin' that he makes some of the big high mens mad by something he done, and so they put chains around his ankles and made him dig a stump in the hot sun. He wasn't used to that 'cause he ain't never done no work in the sun. It gives him the fever to the brain, and he dies.

When Mr. Cramer goes away, Miss Lizzie takes us all and goes back to Old Man Denman's. The sojers used to pass, and all the whoopin', and hollerin', and carryin' on you ain't never heard the likes. They hollers, "Who-oo-oo-oo, Old Man Denman, how's your chickens?" And they chunks and throws at them 'til they cripples them up and can put them in they bags for cookin'. Old Man Denman cusses at them something powerful.

Just like chaps like to do, my sister Mandy and I was down in the woods a fur piece from the house and from the field where Pa and the other mens are hoeing in the fields. We keep hearing a noise, but we thinks it is the men singin' in the fields. Mandy goes to the house to get her vittles and is going to bring me some. She don't never come back. I waits and waits, and finally my brother comes down in the woods and finds me. He says, "Come over to the gate and get your dinner." When I gits there, the dinner is on top of the gate post, and he says they is sojers in the woods atwixt here and the house, and they has been persecutin' a old woman on a mule. She was a nigger woman. I gits so scared, I can't eat my dinner. I ain't got no heart for vittles. My brother says, "Wait for Pa. He is coming with the mule." I gits on the mule in front of Pa, and we passes through the sojers. They grabs at us, and say, "Gimme the gal. Gimme the gal." Pa says I fainted plumb away.

We heard guns shootin' 'round and abouts all the time. Seems like they fit [fought] every time they git a chance. Afore the war is over, the boy of Old Man Denman gits killed. Two of my sisters were his property, and now they don't know what is to be done 'cause they has to be somebody's property, and they ain't no one to 'heritance [inherit] them.

They has to go to the auction, but Old Man Denman says not to worry and not to fret. At the auction, the man says, "Going high, going low, going mighty slow, a little while to go. Bid 'em in, bid 'em in. The sun is high, the sun is hot, and we got to get home tonight." When my sisters is put on the block, an old friend of Old Man Denman's hollers out that he buys for William Blackstone. We all comes home, and Old Man Denman laughs big and says, "My name is always been William Blackstone Denman."

I was a woman growned when the war was to an end. I had my first baby when I was fourteen. One day my sister was in the house, and she calls me and she says, "Theys fit out, and theys been a surrenderin', and they ain't going to fight no more." That dusk Old Man Denman calls all the niggers together, and he stands on the steps and makes a speechin'. He says, "Mens and womens, you is free. You is free as I am. You is free to go where you wants, but I is beggin' you to stay by me 'til we gits the crops laid by. Study it over afore you gives me your answer. I is always tried as my duty to be fair with you."

The men talked it atwixt themselves, and they included to stay. They said we might as well stay here as to go somewhere else. We ain't got no money, and no place to go unless we go a-seekin' a place.

Miss Mizzie married with Mr. Joe McMahon, and I went with her to where she lives not so far by. Mr. McMahon says he is going to learn me how to plow. Miss Lizzie says, "Now, Julia, don't go to the field and make no fool of yourself. Act like you ain't never seen no plow afore. 'Cause you is seen plenty plowin' afore." He learns me, and I learns to hold the handles like this, instead of like that, right down the middle of the furrow, and we made a corn crop.

We goes on about the same, 'cept they don't never seem to be no money, like when my pa used to take a chicken to the town and bring back sweets and little bright things for us chillun.

I got married later on that very year, and I had a little fixin' for the weddin'. Baked some cakes, and I had a dress with buttons, and a preacher married us. I ain't used to wearin' nothin' but lorins [a simple one-piece garment made from sacking]. Underwear? I ain't never wore no underwear then.

After a little while, my husband rents a little piece of land. We moved to it, and raise a corn crop, and that is the way we do. We raises our own vittles on the farm. I had seventeen chilluns through the years. Co'se all of them don't live past being babies and little chilluns. They done scattered to the four winds. Some of them is dead.

I ain't what I used to be for workin'. I can't do much these days but set around. I know, I ain't so long for this world. I done plenty work in my primer days.

Jeptha "Doc" Choice

Jeptha "Doc" Choice, 1117 Brashear Street, Houston, Texas, was born in slavery, October 17, 1835, on the plantation of Jezro Choice, located about six miles south of the present city of Henderson, Texas. Being well liked by his master, Jeptha was given a rudimentary education, attending the plantation school with the white children, and learning to read and write. After the Civil War, Jeptha, thirty years old and no longer a slave, wanted a better education, and Colonel Jones, ex-Confederate officer, son-in-law of Jeptha's former master, paid twenty-five cents weekly to a nearby school for the negro's tuition, the pupil advancing through "fractions" and becoming, according to his own statement, a "sure 'nuff college nigger." Jephta then taught school for several years. He moved to Houston in 1888 and opened a barbershop, one of two in the city at that time. Advanced years forced him to give this up, and he has since practiced "divine healing" among members of his race. In spite of his extreme age, Jeptha, or "Doc" as he is more familiarly known, has an exceptionally clear mind and retentive memory for past events during his lifetime. His pronunciation is also quite good, although at times his speech drops back into typical Negro dialect for a word or phrase.

Yes, suh, I'll be 102 years old come fall, 'cause I was bo'n October 17, 1835, and that's the truth. My mother told me that was the date, and I reckon she know; and beside', I was grown up befo' the war.

We belonged to the Choices, Old Massa Jezro and the missus, I don't remember her name. We niggers all called her the old misssus, and I was bo'n on their plantation, six miles south of where Henderson now is. 'Course, at that time there warn't no town there. The massa and missus had three children, and I was named after one of the boys, Jeptha. I don't recall the other children's names, but one was a girl—and she married Colonel Jones, what took care of me right after the war, when things were mighty tough for us niggers.

My mother's name was Martha. She had been brought here from Serbia, and my father's name was John. He was from the East Indies. They was brought to this country in a slave boat owned by Captain Adair, and sold at New O'leans to someone, I don't recollect Mama telling me who, befo' they belonged to Massa Jezro. I 'member Mamma telling me the old massa liked them, and let them "jump ovah the brom" ["jump over the broom," which was a reference to marriage ceremony], and I was the first child. I had five sisters and one brother, but they is all dead 'ceptin' my brother, who lives up near Henderson. I think I hear Mamma tell that her folks lived in Albino.

Old Massa Jezro was a right kind one and treated us good. He had fifty or sixty slaves, and besides the plantation, he had a gristmill and a tannery.

I recollec' hearing the womenfolks say that befo' I was bo'n some stars fell in April or May—fifteenth of April or fifteenth of May in 1835, about a year befo' the Texas War. Where the stars fell, they set fire to all the small stuff on the ground, like chaff and straw, and the old nigger folks thought that the world was comin' to the end.

My white folks was pretty good to me, and sorta picked me out. You see, if a nigger was smart and showed promise, he was taught how to read and write, and I went to school with the white children on the plantation. Once in a while, Old Massa would take me along to Nacogdoches, and would give me five or ten cents for soda water or candy. When we got back, I sure would be uppity to them other young niggers. I went to the fields when I was about twenty years old, but I didn't have to do much field work, 'cause they was keepin' me good, and they didn't want to strain me. In puttin'-in time in the spring and pickin' time in the fall, the most slaves went out to the field as soon as it was light, and got in at sundown. During in-between times, it was easier. The men worked every day except Saturday afternoon and Sundays. The womenfolks had Saturday off to wash clothes and do the cleanin'.

On Sundays, we'd just put a ol' Prince Albert coat on some good nigger and make a preacher out of him. The white folks was mostly Methodists, and sometimes they would listen to our preachin's, and sorta keep an eye on us thataway.

We niggers had our band, too, and I was one of the players. They was a nigger by the name of Ole Man Tout, the "Conjoor," who could play the violin just as good as anyone you hear today. I don't know why he was called Conjoor, except that he never had to do any hard work and was always around the big house. If anyone would say, "I think we'll send Ole Man Tout to the fields today, the old missus would say, "No, the day is too warm, and the work too hard for the old man. He'll stay at the house," and sure 'nuff, he would.

'Course, sometimes the niggers in the field would get o'nry and not work good, but the overseer on our place wasn't 'lowed to whup. At night, when they came in, he would tell the old massa what the trouble was about, and then the massa would whup the nigger what he thought deserved. Our massa had a tree he tied a bad nigger to to whup him, but some white folks had ring posts and tied a nigger around the neck with a rope— and run the rope through the ring—and tied him up like a mule to whup him.

Then, in the fields was always a big strong nigger to keep peace among the hands. He was called by the other slaves "nigger traitor" behind his back, and was sorta like a straw-boss man. He had to be good with his fists to make the boys who got bad in the field walk the line. 'Course when Old Massa come to the field, anyone who was actin' up started right in to choppin', and everything would get quiet as could be.

The old massa was mighty careful about the raisin' of healthy nigger families, and used us strong, healthy young bucks to stand the healthy young gals. You see, when I was young, they took care not to strain me, and I was a pretty good nigger, as handsome as a speckled pup, and I was much in demand for breedin'. You see, in those days people seemed to know more about such things than they do now. If a young, scrawny nigger was found foolin' 'round the women, he was whupped, and maybe sold.

Later on, we good strong niggers was 'lowed to marry. The massa and old missus would fix the nigger and gal up in new clothes and have the doin's at the big house. White folks would all gather 'round in a circle with the nigger and gal in the center. Then Old Massa would lay a broom down on the floor in front of 'em and tell 'em to join hands and jump over the broom. That married 'em for good.

When babies was bo'n, old nigger grannies handles 'most all them cases, but until they was about three years old, the children warn't 'lowed 'round our regular living quarters, but were wet nursed by nigger women, who did not work in the field and kept in separate quarters. In the evenin', the mammies were let to see them.

'Course, when anything bad in sickness turned up, a doctor would be sent for, but for ordinary sick folks, roots and herbs was most the medicine used, until they brung in drugs from over the water. Befo' the war, they used mostly bitter-apple root and blue mass pills [a preparation of metallic mercury and other ingredients, used for making blue pill]. After the war, quinine was brought in from over the ocean.

Once in a while, Old Massa would send some niggers to another plantation to help with the crops, and would give them a furlough, so that when they were off the plantation they would not be stopped by white folks and whupped. Iffen Old Massa hear of anyone who he let to borrow his niggers mistreatin' 'em, he never would loan them to him no more.

Old Massa used to feed us good, too, and they was lots of beef and hogs on the plantation, and lots of wild game, too. 'Possum and sweet yams is mighty good. You fix it this way—first parboil a 'possum 'bout half done, and then put him in a skewer pan. You know what one of them are? Then put the 'possum in a red-hot oven, and a little while befo' he is done, lay the yams in the pan and sprinkle a little sugar over them and cook them together a little while longer. Then, Cap'n, you has a feast!

Sometime at mealtime when they was short of bread at the house, the old missus would say, "What about some ashcakes?" Ashcakes is what we called them—plain ashcakes. The women-folks would take cornmeal and mix it with water, sometimes they would put in a little milk, but mostly plain water. That's why they was called plain ashcakes. Then they would sweep away the ashes from in front of the big open ha'th [hearth] and put the ashcakes on the hot coals to bake. When they was done, they would sweep the ashes off 'em—and there they was!

'Course sometime they was grief, too, when some of the niggers was sold. Iffen Old Massa sold a nigger man that was married, he always tried to sell the wife to the same white folks, so they would not be separated. Children under twelve were thrown in. But sometimes, a nigger would be sold to someone, and the woman to someone else. Then they'd be carryings-on. But they was so 'fraid of getting whupped, or maybe killed, that they went pretty peaceful-like—but mighty sorrowful. The children went with the mother.

I stayed with my white folks right through the war, but the old massa and his boys joined the South army, and they was all killed. I was in the home guard, which was to protect the old missus and the other womenfolks. The old massa wouldn't take any of us niggers along, 'cause he said this was a white man's fight.

After the war, some Federal provost officers on horseback came to the plantation and told the old missus to call everybody up to the house, and then read a proclamation saying that we niggers was as free as our masters, and not to work anymore unless we got paid for it—and that if we wanted to, we could have land free to farm. This was in July 1865. I did not have any place else to go, so I stayed and helped put up the crops.

That fall, Colonel Jones, who married the old massa's daughter, came home from the war. The reason he did not get back sooner was because he had been wounded in the hospital.

It was pretty tough on niggers for a while. The white folks what was left was mostly womenfolks, and they hadn't no money. Then the Kluxes was bad on niggers, too, and they and some young white men would whup niggers 'til the Federals told them iffen they didn't stop that, they would shoot them. After that it wasn't so bad.

They didn't whup or bother me, 'cause Colonel Jones sorta took care of me, and when he went to live in Henderson, took me with him. Then he paid twenty-five cents a week for more schoolin' for me, and I learned through fractions. When I learned them, I was rated a sure 'nuff college nigger.

Then I got me a job teachin' school. The schools in them times went about six months, and in off times I would farm some, and help keep niggers out of trouble, 'cause on account of my learnin', and not usin' tobacco or drinking, I was kinda boss among the niggers, and the white folks liked me, too.

Well, then, I did lots of different kinds of work—worked on the narrer g'age [narrow gauge] railroad out of Longview; farmed some more, and did lots of other work.

I learnt to be a barber, too, and come to Houston in 1888 and started a barbershop. They was only one or two barbershops here when I come. That was the longest steady work I ever done; but I had to quit a few years back, 'cause I can't stand up for so long no more. Now, I'm tryin' to help my people by divine healin', and tellin' them the right way to live.

I've been married eight times but haven't got any legitimate children that I know. I've got some children from outside women I've had to stand for, but I don't know how many. You see, them old days was different from what it is now.

Millie Williams

Millie Williams, age eighty-six, lives at 1612 East Fourth Street, Fort Worth, Texas. She was born a slave to Joe Benford, in Tennessee, and was sold to Bill Dunn, who brought her to Texas and traded her to Tommy Ellis for some land. She has lived in Fort Worth since the 1870s.

I don't know when I was born, 'cause I was taken from my folks when I was a baby, but Massa told me I was born in the spring of the year in 1851. I was born on Massa Benford's place in Tennessee, and my mama's name was Martha Birdon. She say my pappy's name Milton Cade, but I never seed him. And I didn't know my mama a long time, 'cause she's sold away from Massa Benford's place, and I was sold with her. Then he took me back, and I never seed my mama no mo'.

After I was sold back to Massa Benford, he puts me in the nigger yard. That where the massa kept slaves what he traded. It was just a bunch of shacks throwed together, and dirty was no name for it, it was worse than a pigpen. The man what watch

Millie Williams

over us in that nigger yard was the meanest man what ever lived. He'd take a club and beat the daylight out of us, 'cause the club wouldn't leave scars like the bullwhip, and didn't bring the price down when we is sold.

One day Massa Benford takes us to town and puts us on that auction block, and a man name Bill Dunn bought me. I was 'bout seven years old. Talkin' 'bout somethin' awful, you should have been there. The slave owners was shoutin' and sellin' chillen to one man and the mama and pappy to 'nother. The slaves cries and takes on somethin' awful. If a woman had lots of chillen she was sold for mo', 'cause it a sign she a good breeder.

Right after I was sold to Massa Dunn, there was a big uprisin' in Tennessee, and it was 'bout the Union. I don't know what it was all about, but they wanted Massa Dunn to take some kind of oath, and he wouldn't do it, and he had to leave Tennessee. He said they would take the slaves 'way from him, so he brought me and Sally Armstrong to Texas. There he trades us to Tommy Ellis for some land, and that Massa Ellis, he the best white man what ever lived. He was so good to us, we was better off than when we's free.

Massa Ellis's plantation was one of the biggest, and he owned land as far as we could see. There was 'bout fifty slaves, and we lived in a row of log cabins 'long side the big house. In winter, we sleeps inside, but in summer we sleeps in the yard, and the same 'bout eatin'. Sometimes Massa fed good, and then 'gain he didn't, but that 'cause of the war. We has cornbread, and milk, and all the coffee you would drink. On Sundays, we fills the pot half full of meat and shell peas on top the meat.

I 'member the time we steals one of Massa's big chickens, and it's in the pot in the fireplace when we seed Missy comin'. I grabs that chicken and pot and puts it under the bed and puts the bedclothes top that pot. Missy, she come in and say, "I sho' do smell somethin' good." I say, "Where, Missy Ellis?" She don't find nothin', so she leaves. When she's gone, I takes that chicken, and we eats it in a hurry.

The overseer woke 'em up 'bout four in the mornin', but I works in the house. The field workers gets off Thursdays and Saturday evenin's, and Sunday. The reason they gets off Thursdays is that Massa has some kind of thought we shouldn't work that day. Maybe it was 'ligion, I don't know.

We has parties and sings:

> Massa sleeps in the feather bed,
> Nigger sleeps on the floor;
> When we'uns gets to Heaven,
> They'll be no slaves no mo'.

Then we has the song 'bout this:

> Rabbit in the briar patch,
> Squirrel in the tree,
> Wish I could go huntin',
> But I ain't free.

> Rooster's in the hen house,
> Hen's in the patch,
> Love to go shootin',
> But I ain't free.

When the nigger leaves the plantation without no pass, and the patterollers caught him, they gives him thirty-nine licks with the bullwhip. When we's in the fields and sees the patteroller ride by, we starts murmurin' out loud, "Patter the pat, patter the pat!" One after 'nother took it up, and purty soon everybody mummerin'. We do that to let everybody know the patteroller 'round.

When war start, there a army camp just below the plantation and 'bout a thousand soldiers. We hears 'em shout, "Halt. March. Halt. March," all day long. They sung:

> Lincoln's not satisfied,
> He wants to fight 'gain.
> All he got to do,
> Is hustle up his men.

I stays with Massa Ellis after we's freed. There sho' was a mighty party when the slaves knows they's free. They hug one 'nother and almost tear their clothes off. Some cryin' for the husband, and some cryin' for the chillen.

When I was 'bout twenty, I left Massa's home and moves to Dallas, where I marries my first man. His name was Bill Jackson. He left me and goes back to Dallas. I hear he die, so I marry Will Williams, and he dies. Now I been here since the Lord know when.

Millie Ann Smith

*Millie Ann Smith was born in Rusk County, Texas, in 1850, as a
slave of George Washington Trammell, a pioneer planter and
financier of Rusk County. Her mother was originally from Mississippi and her father from Alabama. Trammell bought Millie's
mother and three older children in Mississippi before Millie was
born and brought them to Texas. Millie moved with her mother to
the home of a white widow-lady four years after the war, and lived
there until she married. She reared five children to be grown. Since
the death of her husband she has lived alone in Sunny South
addition in Marshall and now draws an eight-dollar-per-month
pension from the government.*

I was bo'n 'fore the war started and 'members when it
ceased. I guess Mammy's folks allus belonged to the Trammells. I
'member my grandfather, Josh Chiles, and my grandmother,
Jeanette Chiles. I was a strappin' big girl when they died. I 'member my grandfather say he come to Texas with Master George
Trammell's father when Rusk County was just a "big woods," and
that the first two years he was a hunter for his master. He say he

Millie Ann Smith

in the woods all the time killing deer, wild hogs, turkeys, coons, and the like for the white fo'ks to eat. He say the land was full of Indians when they come to Texas. He kinda took up with them and had holes in his nose and ears put there by the Indians for the rings they wore in their nose and ears. He could talk most any Indian language. He say he used to run off from his master and stay with the Indians weeks at a time. His master would go to the Indian camp looking for him, and the Indians hided him out and say "No see him."

My grandmother Jeanette was baptized by a white preacher and joined the white chu'ch. She wore a white muslin dress that her mistress fixed for her. She used to show it to us and tell us how she loved her mistress. She kept her "baptizing dress" 'til she died and was buried in it.

When Master George Washington Trammell, my master, come to Texas with his wife and three chil'ren, he brought my mother and her three chil'ren. Pappy belonged to a George Moore there in Mississippi, and Master Trammell hadn't bought him when we left to come to Texas. Pappy run off and come to Texas and begged Master into buying him, so he could be with his wife and chil'ren.

Master George and Mistress America didn't have no chil'ren but raised two of Mistress's sister's girls. They lived in a big fine house, owned more slaves and land than anybody in Rusk County, and was 'bout the riches folks I knowed of. The slaves lived down the hill from Master's house in a double row of log cabins. My grandfather Josh made all the beds for the white folks, and the niggers, too. They was decent to sleep on. Master didn't want anything shoddy 'round him, not even his nigger quarters.

We raised rice, wheat, cane, and everything there on the place. Master had a big garden where we got peas, beans, and garden-truck. The niggers didn't have no time to fool with gardens.

I's sot [sat] all day handing thread to Mammy to put in the loom. They give us homespun clothes, and you'd better keep them if you didn't want to go naked. On Christmas, Master would fetch us down flour, syrup, sugar, and fresh meat so we could have gingerbread cake.

Master had an overseer and a nigger-driver named Jacob Green, but he 'lowed no one to whip one of his niggers but hisself. If one was hard to control he was tied to a tree. Some of the bosses tied them down 'cross a barrel and beat them might' nigh to death. I give justice to Master Trammell, he didn't do nothing like that, but allus call us up and talk to us and then whip us right. Master didn't have no chil'ren of his own. It was the white folks that had a passel of chil'ren that was so hard on them, and worked them nearly to death. Them what had a bunch of chil'ren would 'cuse [accuse] the niggers of doing something to them so they could whip them.

We was woke up 'fore daybreak with a horn and wo'ked til sundown. When we got in from the field, there was stock to tend to, and chores to do, and cloth to weave 'fore we went to bed. The overseer come 'round at nine o'clock to see if we was in bed, then he go back to the house and run in. When we knowed he was sound 'sleep we slip out and run 'round, and go to the neighbors sometimes. We warn't 'lowed to go to chu'ch, or nowhere without a pass. I think sometime, how we did live through it? The Lord took care of us.

They locked young men up in a house on the place at night and on Sunday to keep them from running 'round. It was a log house and had cracks in it. One time a little nigger boy was sticking his hand through the crack poking fun at the boys on the inside and one of them chopped his fingers off with an ax.

Master Trammell didn't 'low no nigger on the place what could read and write if he knowed it. George Wood was the only one of his slaves I knowed of that could read and write. A little white boy that belonged to some fo'ks on a 'joining place took up with George 'cause he would play with him. They went off in the woods, and the boy showed George how to read and write. Master didn't find out 'bout it 'til after Freedom.

The white fo'ks had a chu'ch four or five miles off the place. Precious little we went as Master Trammell's fo'ks—only went on "big meeting" days. We slipped off and had prayer meetings and prayed to ourselves but darsn't let the white fo'ks know 'bout it. We hummed our religious songs in the field while we was wo'king. It was our way of praying for Freedom, but the white fo'ks did not know it. My favorite spiritual went like this . . . I don't recalls all of it:

> Am I bo'n to die to lay this body down?
> Must my trembling spirit fly into world unknown,
> The land of deepest shades only pierced
> > by human thought.

Master Trammell give the niggers a tract of new ground to a family. He 'lowed them Saturday afternoon and to twelve o'clock nights to work the land. They cleared it up, planted it, and got what they made off it the first year. Master would take the cotton they raised to Shreveport to sell it and bring us back calico, plaid, and nice cloth for clothes, and everything else we wanted. He give the old fo'ks the money that was left after he bought what they wanted. Grandpappy Josh made money selling wild turkey and hogs to the poor white fo'ks. Master let them go hunting at night and kill turkeys, hogs, and other game to sell.

We had our medicine in slavery time. The old women made it out of weeds and things from the woods. We took blue mass [a preparation of metallic mercury and other ingredients, used for making blue pills], Everlasting Life [more commonly known as Life Everlasting], boneset horsemint tea, butterfly weed teas, and Jerusalem oak, and bottled it up for the winter. Butterfly weed tea was good for the pleurisy. The other are remedies for chills, fever, and sick-like. As regular as I got up, I allus drank my asfidity and tar water.

I's seen a 150 hands on one pile of corn at corn shuckings. They pile it up in windrows and call in the hands from all 'round. The women cooked up chicken stews, tater custard, pies, and all kinds of meat and vegetables. Master come 'round now and then and give the men a drink. The chil'ren whooped and hollered, while the men and women shucked co'n.

On Saturday nights Master made us gang up, and sing, and dance, and play ring plays. Our favorite was "Eleven Stars, Eleven Stars Gwine to Fall," "Gwine Up North, Newbound Wearing Broadcloth," and "Chickens Crowing for Midnight, It's Almost Day."

I 'member when the war was going on, Trammell furnished three of his slaves— Ed Chile, Jacob Green, and Job Jester as mule skinners for the war. I seed tho government come to Trammell's place and take off a big bunch of mules. 'Most on to four years after the war, three men come to Master's and made him call us up and turn us loose. He told us we could work on for wages. That's the first we knowed 'bout being free. I saw a bunch of soldiers marching by the place long time after the war started and asked Mammy where they was going. She say the war was over. My father went to work for wages after Trammell turn us loose, and my mother went to keep house for a widow white lady. I stayed there with her 'til I married.

Monroe Brackins

*Monroe Brackins was born in Monroe County, Mississippi, in 1853,
the property of George Reedes. With his father, mother, and two
sisters, he was brought to Medina County, Texas, at the age of two.
His master settled first at a place called Malone, on the Hondo
River, later moving to the Adams Ranch, twenty miles down river,
where Monroe learned the art of snaring and breaking mustangs
and became an expert cowpuncher. After Freedom, he followed this
vocation until fences closed up the country, and there was no free
range nor wild cattle left. While a cowboy, he knew Big Foot Wallace
and used to listen to that famous frontiersman spin yarns. About
1890, when the old style of ranching began to die out, Monroe
bought a farm of eighty acres on the Tywauknay, where he lived
until 1934. In that year, he sold the farm and moved his house to
Hondo, where he is now living in a crude unscreened building.*

I was born in Mississippi, Monroe County. I am eighty-four
years old. George Reedes brought me to Texas when I was two
years old. He brought my mother, and father, and two sisters,
and me.

My father was Nelson Brackins, and my mother was Rosanna,

Monroe Brackins

but I couldn't tell you her name before she was married. I have a sister in this county. Lost three; one died here last year—Sarah Ann Grant, Austin Grant's wife. One sister was named Ellen, and one named Rosie. No brothers. I declare, I didn't remember where they said they were bo'n, but we came here from Mississippi to Texas. My father had been all back in those old states there. I heard him speak of North Ca'lina and Lou'siana.

He [Reedes] first settled here at a place we called the Malone on the Hondo River. They lived there for awhile, and then they moved away from there. He come here and went into stock business when he came from Mississippi. Our house here [after they came from Mississippi] was a little old picket house with a grass roof over it out of the sage grass. The bed was a kind of . . . the tickin', I think, was shucks, and the children slept on the floor. The boss's house was just a common house. The first house that they had was just a little lumber house, but that wasn't their own property, and they moved later on. He taken us about twenty miles fu'ther down on the Hondo, the Old Adams' Ranch, at the rock house. He stayed in the stock business, raising stock. He was a big stock man. Cattle mostly.

I was then six years old, but not big enough to do any work. I learned the stock business principally on the Adams' Ranch. They stayed there quite awhile. After I got large enough, I was a horse breaker. We thought it [horse breaking] was alright. We had regular Spanish horses and some real broncos. We had shoes. I had to have some kind of shoes, because they had me in the brush nearly all the time, and I had to have something to keep the thorns out of my feet. I wore rawhide leggin's, too. I'll tell you, lady, we just had such clothes as we could get—old, patched-up clothes. They just had that jeans cloth, homemade clothes—pants, and jackets, and such-like. I was with George Reedes probably ten or twelve years. It was my first training—with George

Reedes—learnin' the stock business and horse breakin'.

He was tolerable good to us, to be slaves as we were. Tolerable good after we come to Texas. George's brother, John, had a hired man that whipped me once. He just whipped me with a quirt [a riding whip consisting of a short, stout stock and a lash of braided leather]. I have heard my father and mother tell how they whipped 'em in Mississippi. They'd tie 'em down, on a log or up to a post, and whip 'em 'til the blisters rose, then take a paddle and open 'em up and pour salt in 'em. Well, if they had treated 'em [the slaves] right, there wouldn't have been any war. John and Bill Reedes took my father and my father's old partner over to Mexico during the war and told 'em they were as free as they were themselves, and to stay if they wanted to, but my father and his fellow servant came on back with 'em, instead of stayin'. They were freighting cotton over there, and of course, they had families, and they wanted to come back to them. I never would go to Mexico.

They whipped the women. The most I remember about that— my father and sister was in the barn shucking co'n, and this Bill Reedes—there were four brothers living on the same plantation —Bill Reedes, he came in there and was whipping my sister with a cowhide whip. He missed her, and my father caught the lick in the face, and he told Bill Reedes if he was goin' to whip Nancy to keep his whip off of him. That insulted Bill Reedes, and he commenced on him, and he [his father] run away. When he finally did come in, he was so wild his master tried to call him in to get orders for work. But he [his father] sent word to come *there*. Finally the boss shot at him to scare him, and they finally get him worked back, but they didn't whip him any more. Of course, some of 'em whipped with more mercy. It [whippings] didn't happen very often on our place.

The white people we was raised up with had a pretty good

education and used pretty good language. That's why I don't talk like most cullud folks. What little I got into—I was grown, and there was an English family settled close, about one-half mile, I guess. They had a little boy, his name was Arthur Ederle, and he come over there and learned me how to spell "cat" and "dog" and "hen" and such-like. I was right around about twenty years old. I couldn't sign my name when I was eighteen years old.

I don't remember scarcely anything about the war because I was so little, and times was so different then. The country wasn't settled up, and everything was wild—no people, hardly. Of course, my life was in the woods, you might say, didn't know when Sunday hardly came. We lived among the Indians and wild beast. I've heard folks say that the white folks crossed up with the culluds, and they would even sell their own children. Of course, the North couldn't stand it. The Northern soldiers never did get down in here, that I know of. So far as we knew, there wasn't any war goin' on—only just what we could hear of. I know once, when they was enlisting men to go to the battle, a whole lot 'em that didn't want to fight would run away and dodge out, and our Southern people would follow 'em and try to make 'em fight. They had a battle up here on the Nueces once and killed out some of 'em. I know my boss was in the bunch that followed some of 'em, and I know he got scared up for fear this old case would be brought up after the war. The company that followed these men called the Old Duff Company. I think there was somewhere around forty in the bunch they followed, but I don't know how many they killed. There was a big bluff and a big water hole, and they claimed that they were throwed in that big water hole.

I was somewhere around about six or seven years old when the slaves were freed. After the war, we worked for George Reedes awhile, then we drifted on down to the Frio [River] and stayed there about a year. Then we come back to Medina County and settled down here close to where I was raised, below the Reedes place.

We didn't consider it hard times at all right after the war. The country was wild and unsettled, with ranches fifteen or twenty miles apart. You never did see anybody, and so we didn't know really what was goin' on in the rest of the country. Sometimes somethin' could happen in five miles of us, and we didn't know it for a month.

We had 'possums and 'coons to eat sometimes. My father was very fond of 'coons. There was plenty of rabbits. My father, he generally cooked the 'coons. He would dress 'em and stew and bake 'em. My mother wouldn't have anything to do with 'em, because she didn't eat 'em. Sometimes when they had potatoes, they cooked 'em with 'em [raccoons]. They didn't raise potatoes every year. Reedes was a cow-ranch man. I can remember one time they had just a small patch of blackhead sugar cane. After the Freedom, she [his mother] had a kind of garden. She planted snap beans and —well, I guess she raised watermelons pretty much all of the time.

He [Reedes] fed us tolerable well. Everythin' was wild. Beef was free; just had to bring one in and kill it. Once in awhile, of a Sunday mornin', we'd get biscuit bread to eat. It was quite a treat to us. They measured the flour out, and it had to put out just like they measured. He gave us a little somethin' good to eat. I heard my people say that coffee was high, at times, and I know that we didn't get no flour, only on Sunday mornin'. We live on co'nbread, mostly; beef and game out of the woods. That was durin' the war, and a short time after the war, also.

I was on the Adams ranch on the Hondo, and my master came out and told us that we were as free as he was. When he came out and told us, there were four of us freed. He said we could stay on and work, or we could go if we wanted to. He gave my father and mother, I think, fifty cents apiece and twenty-five cents for the chil'ren. We stayed awhile, and then went west to Frio. I don't know whether he paid them anything after they were freed, just what they had.

I used to be along with Old Man Big Foot Wallace in my early days. He was a might' fine man. Just on his ranch—I didn't exactly work for him, but I worked for the people that were gathering stock together there. Big Foot raised nice horses, old reg'lar Texas horses, but they were better than the reg'lar old Spanish broncos. I used to go to his camp down on the San Miguel. He had a little camp down there. He lived in one part, and his chickens in the other part of his house. It was a kind of a long house he had fixed up. They [Big Foot's friends] always like to be in his company to hear him talk about his travels. I don't know how come him to stop in there. He used to run stock horses, and a figger [figure] seven on the left shoulder for his brand and the tip of each ear was his earmark. I never heard of any extra ridin' he done. I never saw him on anything but a gentle horse. He wasn't a very heavy man. He got that name from the Indians. His feet was just a little larger than the Indians.

I didn't follow the Indians with Big Foot, but I did with my master's bunch. I was in one battle with the Indians. They were using bows and arrows, and they could shoot pretty good, if the wind wasn't strong. All the Indians were wild that I saw, except one boy they captured, and a man raised him. I saw that boy a few times. My master taken me for about forty miles, and it was on the ranch where this boy was. He seemed to be about like one of these Meskin [Mexican] boys here. Of course, he was civil. He talked English. I suppose he knew he wasn't an Indian. The worst part of living down in this country was we had to be like chickens watching for hawks. We had to watch for Indians and such dangers as rattlesnakes and the like.

On a stock ranch, we would take up a horse and break him as we took 'em up, and train 'em as we went along. It taken awhile to get one trained. Sometimes there would be two or three we would take up and break during a month, but sometimes just one. I was pretty good with a rope. Yes, I can say I had a pretty good practice with a rope. I never had to hunt a ranch to work on. There was someone always ready for me, on account of being a good cowhand. I used to help on the roundups here, and help with the herds 'til they were ready to go to the trail, but I didn't go. That night guarding and the hard life didn't appeal to me.

The last man I broke horses for was Wilson Bailey. I was with him about twelve years. He said it was a pity for us old fellows to get old, because we had such practice and knew so much about it. He raised just cavi-yard. We just said a cavi-yard of horses, just the same thing as a *remuda* [a herd of saddle horses]. We called them a *remuda* later, but we got that from the Spanish.

We would get in a tree with our loop 'til he [a horse] come under and drop it down on him. When they were so spoilt, we would get 'em in a sort of cavi-yard and drive 'em under the trees and snare 'em. We had lots of them [wild horses] in here, just this side of Pearsall, then we would cut some mesquite stakes and cut brush and weave it between the stakes. Some wings would be fifty yards long or more. Whenever we wanted to catch some mustangs, we built a corral and the wings, generally close to a water hole. The owner of the place used 'em for cow ponies.

Once in a great while, I got throwed. Once in awhile; not very often. 'Bout the only way I'd get throwed was to get careless and be off guard. We'd catch him and let him go. Sometimes they would be too wild to pitch. They'd break and run, and you had to let him run himself down. Most of the cowboys took it for fun then, or pleasure. I used to rather catch a wild horse and break him than to eat breakfast. A person didn't have to be nervous, if he wanted to stick on him. After I got on a pitchin' horse—after I got good practice—I used my quirt all over him to make him give up. Some of 'em will pitch, and you get 'em good broke, and turn 'em out, and let 'em get grass-fat, and he will pitch worse than ever.

We would buy our rope and make hackamore [rope bridles used for breaking horses], but when first used 'em the Meskins brought 'em from Mexico. That's where we got our idea. They made their hackamores out of horsehair. At that time, we made lariats out of rawhide. They were better than grass ropes, and didn't burn your hand, and was better to rope with. When they were greased a few times, they would get mightly pliant. [Interviewer's note: Monroe says they learned of their cowboy lore from the Mexicans, who, he says, were experts.]

Now, Bill Reedes went off to the war, but he wasn't killed, and came back, and married later on. Well, after we moved back to Medina County, between the Medina and Hondo [Rivers], what we called Black Creek, I followed the life of a cowboy and horse breaker 'til there wasn't any cattle left, and they began fencing up the country, putting it into pasture. Then I had to go to farmin'. I knew of Old Man White and knew about his settlement. [Interviewer's note: This reference is to a Negro slave settlement, laid off in farms and sold to them by a man named White.] When I first commenced farmin', I taken up some state land—they called it vacant land—about eighty acres. That was down on Black Creek, but in Medina County. I stayed on that place a number of years—I can't say just how many years, but I was on that place ten or twelve years. I farmed most of it, though there was no fences down there. Twenty-five acres would have been a very large farm at that time. I raised some corn, sugar cane, and watermelons. When I first commenced farmin', cotton hadn't got into this country. I eventually raised cotton. I commenced with horses, but long way down the line. I used oxen some, too. I owned about two yoke of oxen, or one pair, and I used one of those old walking plows. Such implements as we have now wasn't produced here. Didn't even have double shovels.

I sold the Black Creek place and moved to the place on Tywaukney [Interviewer's note: Tonkawa?—spelling not on local maps] Creek or Branch. I began to come up to this settlement to church and to entertainments, and I met my wife then. Her name was Ida Bradley. I was thirty-eight years old when I married. I took my wife back down to Tywaukney. We lived down there right about twenty-three years. We raised our family there. I've got three children living. Two died. When we married, we just had a little home weddin'. I wore an ordinary suit. I don't remember the color of the suit she wore. We got married about eight o'clock in the evenin'. Just had a supper. Her folks was strictly members of the church. We had barbecue, cake, and ice cream.

I left the Tywaunkney in 1934 for good. I bought this place here in town, so that I could bring my family here to have the advantage of school. Now I am just livin' here alone. I have a daughter in California, and one of them boys, too. But the oldest one—the last letter I had from him—I believe they call it Center, Texas. The one in California is runnin' a tailor shop, and I think the girl is just a kind of housemaid. My wife died out in California.

Laura Cornish

*Laura Cornish, living at 2915 Nance Street, Houston, Texas, was
born on the plantation of Isaiah Day, near Dayton, Liberty County,
Texas. She does not know just when she was born, but she thinks she
was "'bout twelve or mebbe thirteen years old when all the cullud
folks was turned loose." She also stresses the fact that Mr. Day
would allow no one to refer to the colored people on his plantation
as slaves or "niggers," insisting they were as free and white of soul as
anyone, only "we is darker on the outside 'cause we is sunburnt."*

Lord have mercy 'pon me, when you calls me Aunt Laura it
seems just like you must be some of my white folks, 'cause that's
what they calls me—I mean Papa Day's chillen and their young
'uns when they use to come see me. But it's been a long time
since any of 'em come to see old Aunt Laura, and I reckon they
'most all gone now.

You know where Dayton is at? Well, that's where Papa Day's
plantation was at, and where at I was born. I don't know just
when I was born 'xactly, but when all the cullud folks was turned
loose, you know, when they was freed by the gov'ment, I was

'bout twelve or mebbe thirteen years old.

Mamma's name was Maria Dunlap, and Daddy's name was Saul Dunlap. I don't rec'lect where Mamma come from, but I hear her say it was somewhere here in Texas. She was the seamstress and don't do nothin' but weave cloth on the spinnin' wheel and make clothes. Daddy was from Lake Providence, I hear him say, but I don't know where at that is. He does all the carpenter work 'round the plantation. I has five sisters and two brothers, but they is all lots older'n me and don't pay much mind to me, and that's 'bout all I knows 'bout my own folks. I s'pose Mamma and Daddy has folks, too, but they wasn't on Papa Day's place, and I don't rec'lect hearin' 'em talk 'bout 'em.

We belong to Mr. Day, his name was Isaiah Day, but we all calls him Papa Day 'cause he won't 'low none of his cullud folks to call him master. He says we is born just as free as he is, only the other white folks won't tell us so, and that our souls is just as white, and the reason we is darker on the outside is 'cause we is sunburnt. I has heard of lots of good white folks and some bad white folks, but I don't reckon there was anyone what was as good to the cullud folks as he was.

Miss Martha, that was his wife, was mighty good, too, and do any of us chillen get hurt or scratched, she's the one we goes to, and she fixes us up with ointment or lin'ment, 'pendin' [depending] on what the trouble is. Then she gives us a hug and say, "Now you be careful and not get hurt no more." Lord have mercy, I can hear her just as plain like it was only yesterday. I knows Papa Day has two boys and a girl, and long time ago they come to see me, and brings their own chillen, but I just can't 'member things so well no more. The Lord forgive me, but I just can't rec'lect their names now. Seems like some things I 'members all right, and some things I tries to think of what I has knowed 'bout is kinda foggy-like.

I can't tell now how many cullud folks Papa Day has on the

plantation, but I knowed he had lots of 'em. 'Course I was just young then, and 'bout all I think of was playin' and eatin', and we chillen sure did plenty of both of 'em. The only work Papa Day let us chillen do was in the cotton field in the fall when the cotton was most picked. We picks the bolls close to the ground what was hard for the grown folks to get. That wasn't much work, it's mostly fun, and we gets to ride to the house on the wagon what takes the pickin' in at night.

But I rec'lect 'sides the cotton, Papa Day has lots of sugar cane, and grinds the cane for two or three weeks and makes the sugar and syrup right on the plantation. Then he raises lots of sheep and hogs and cattle, 'cause it takes lots to feed all the folks on the place.

They ain't nobody can tell me they has better white folks then Papa Day. None of his cullud folks works Sattidays and Sundays. They has that time off to do what they wants to, mebbe visit 'round to the neighbor plantations, and we don't have to have no pass like the cullud folks do on the other plantations, I's tellin' you the truth. And no one had better bother us none either, 'cause Papa Day tell everyone if they touch a hair on our head, they better do a good job and kill us, 'cause he's goin' to kill the one what hurts us.

They never was no whippin' on our place neither, 'cause Papa Day say we is human bein's and not beasts.

I rec'lect one time we chillen is playin' out near some woods where they is a big briar patch, and we see two old men what look like wild men sure 'nuff. They had long hair all over their faces, and their shirts was all bloody. When they see us lookin' they hides down in the brush. Lord have mercy, we sure was scairt, and we run as fast as we could to the house and tell Papa Day what we has seen. He tells us to take him on to where we has seen the men, and we goes to the place and sure 'nuff they is still there. Papa Day goes in the briar patch. Me and Lucy, one of the chillen I's playin' with, go 'long, too, but the rest stays out. The old men take Papa Day 'round the knees and begs him not to tell their master where they is at 'cause they get whipped some more and mebbe kilt. Papa Day asks 'em who they belong to, and they say they is Old Lodge and Old Baldo, and they has run 'way 'caused they is old, and their master whips 'em 'cause they can't work so good no more. I don't rec'lect now who they say they belong to, but I 'member Papa Day has tears comin' in his eyes, and he says that is the sin of sins, to bloody flesh that way.

I don't know how long they has hid in the briar patch, but they can't hardly walk. Papa Day sends me to the house and tells me to have Aunt Mandy, the cook, to fix up some food and to hurry and bring it back. Lord have mercy, I never see such eatin', there wasn't 'nough left for an ant to feed hisself, they was so hungry.

That's one time I see Papa Day mad. He tells the old men to stay where they is at 'til he gets back, and we goes to the house and drives down to where the po' old men is at and brung 'em to the house and doctors 'em and gives 'em some clean clothes. Then he tell everybody to mind their own business and not to stand 'round gawkin', and puts Old Lodge and Baldo in a house in the quarters by theyselves, and tells us not to say nothin' to nobody 'bout what we has seen. Then he gets on a horse and rides off and don't get back 'til most dark, and you know what he done when he ride off? He goes to the man what owned Old Lodge and Baldo and tells him they is at our place and just dares him to try and get 'em. Yes, suh, that's the truth 'cause Aunt Mandy hears him tell Miss Martha 'bout it. I hears later on he pays the man somethin' for 'em, 'cause they stays right on our place and work a little 'round the yard. I guess they thought they was in heaven at Papa Day's place.

Now I tells you somethin', and it's the truth, too. From way back to that time to this day, I can't eat no watermelon, 'cause the red meat look just like the bloody shirts of Old Lodge and Baldo, and just to think of it 'bout makes me sick to my stomach. Lord have mercy, they was the awfulest sight I ever see.

In the summertime when it come 'bout eleven o'clock, Papa Day tell Aunt Mandy to ring the bell and call the folks in from the field 'cause the sun was so hot, and they don't go back to the field 'til the sun was on a good slant, neither.

On Sunday we has preachin' on the plantation. Papa Day do the preachin' and 'fore long folks is clappin' hands and shoutin' and singin'. He don't preach none 'bout us obeyin' no white master or mistress, no, suh, but he tell us we better 'bey the teachin' in the Good Book and serve the Lord. I 'members the two songs we sing the most is "Amazin' Grace" and "Am I Born to Die." Lord have mercy, how we all sing and thank the Lord for all the goodness.

One mornin' Papa Day calls all the folks up to the house and reads 'em the freedom papers what the gov'ment says to read to all the cullud folks, and when he finish readin' he say "The gov'ment don't need to tell you that you is free, 'cause you has been free all your days. Now if you wants to stay you can, and if you wants to go you can, but if you go, white folk ain't goin' to treat you like I do." That's just the words what he said.

For the longest time, mebbe two years, they warn't none of Papa Day's cullud folks what left, but then first one fam'ly then 'nother gets 'em some land to make a crop on, and then we leaves too, when Daddy gets him some land.

I don't rec'lect how he gets it, mebbe from Papa Day, 'cause it warn't far from his place, but Daddy and Mamma and me goes to farmin' on it. My sisters and brothers was all older'n me, and they was all married, and Papa Day had married 'em hisself outen the Book. Some of 'em stay and worked for Papa Day, and some had a place of their own, but Daddy and Mamma and me sure worked hard on our place, and I hear Mamma say lots of times she wish we stay on Papa Day's place.

I don't rec'lec' just how long we stay on the farm, but 'members one year we don't make no crop hardly, and Daddy say he goin' to get out 'fore we starves to death, and we comes to Houston. Daddy gets him a job as carpenter and hires me out for a house girl, but I don't stay long 'cause Mamma took sick, and I had to nurse her 'til she die. Then Daddy took sick right after Mamma is buried and died of the rots. I don't 'member what else they calls it what he died from.

Lord have mercy, that sure was a hard time for me when I lose my Mamma and Daddy, and I has to go back to Dayton and stay to my sister Rachel. I's had a hard time since, 'cause both my husbands what I married has been dead a long time, and the only chile I had died when he was just a baby. I's just alone, sittin' and waitin' for the Lord to call me.

Anthony W. Lacy

Anthony W. Lacy, a tall, slender, always neatly dressed Negro, is one of the most highly respected of his race in the county. His dark bronze skin and rather excitable nature undoubtedly descend from the African race, but his intelligence, thin lips, and general profile bespeak a mixture with lighter colored people. His spirit seems to revolt yet at his master's unjust and cruel treatment of his slaves, for he repeated several times the story of his master's saying he never wanted to see any of his old slaves again. He seems thrifty and dependable in all his ways.

I am Anthony W. Lacy. I was bo'n in Jasper County, six mile souf'west of the then little town of Jasper. And I lives yet, right where I was bo'n seventy-five year ago. Joe Trailer was our marster, and he have 'bout a hunnerd slaves, and he make three or fo' hunnerd bale of cotton a year. He what I call one bad marster. You couldn't lay yo' hand on my mudder's [mother's] back but you would hit a stripe. Her task was three hunnerd pounds of cotton a day on half rations, and Fadder's [Father's] was five hunnerd. Fadder offen stay in the woods and woulden take he punishment.

When we was set free, our marster didn't give he niggers a thing. He got up and move to West Texas, and say he was goin' to stay where he couldn't see a free nigger, as they didn't deserve freedom. I don't 'member so much 'bout the war, but my fadder say befo' he come west, you could hear the cannon from Natchez to Lou'siana.

Two and a half pounds of meal was the weekly ration give the slaves, and they work them hard. They was told they better not call for no mo' rations befo' Saddidy [Saturday] night. Marster sell three thousand pounds of cotton for fifty cents a pound just befo' he go west.

Us didn't have no good time 'til after us got free. I's so small, they not bother me much, but when I see them whip Mudder and the other slaves, it skeert me and make my heart so' [sore] at our marster, 'cause he so mean to all them and punish them for most nuttin'.

He git so hard on them that Wade Grimmet, Peter Trailor, and Jan Trailor run 'way and got to the woods and live in caves. You kin see these old caves in the woods yit, where they and other slaves lived.

Fadder was a nat'ral mechanic. Marster was better to Fadder, 'cause he make all they plows, and they have to have 'em. He make some fine plows that they said would have cost two thousand dollar at that time.

In slavery days, there was a white man stay here by the name of Palmer. He make business of huntin' runaway niggers with bloodhound. One day he run some of us neighbor's niggers. One of them jump in the water up to he neck. The dogs come after him, and he cut one of them in two. Then they git him out and make him carry that dog a mile or more, then dress and eat a ham of him. Then they ax him, "Is he good?"

The nigger say, "Yeah, gimme some mo'."

Then they take him and wo' [wore] him 'pletely [completely] out whippin' him.

Us see very little of the war, but I's live right 'bout six mile from Jasper all this seventy-five year of my life. I's come to town 'bout twixt a week to sell my farm produce, and buy stuff at the sto', and have seen many change in this county durin' that time. I see Jasper grow from most nothin' but brush heap to a fine big town. I know most ev'ry body, and they knows me. I's live a good straight life, and most people 'spects [respects] me. I likes Jasper, and it the only home I ever have know, and I well satisfy to stay here 'mong my fren' [friends] where Fadder and Mudder die and be bury.

Josephine Ryles

Josephine Ryles, known to the colored folks around her home at 3505 Avenue, in Galveston, as "Mama Honey," was born a slave in Galveston, Texas. Her mother, Mary Alexander, was the only slave of James Sultry, early Galveston insurance agent. Later they were sold to Tom Snow of Polk County, Texas, and lived there until freed by the Civil War. After the war they returned to Galveston.

Sure, I'm Josephine Ryles. Only everyone 'round here calls me Mama Honey, and I 'most forgot my name 'til you said it just then. Honey, I be glad to tell you all I 'member, 'bout slavery but it ain't much, for my mind ain't so good no more. Sometime I can't 'member nothin' at all. I'm too old. I was born in slavery, but I don't know when. Me and that Gulf got here 'bout the same time I reckon.

I was born in Galveston. James Sultry own us—that is, he own my mother. She was the only one he had. He had a kind of big place on Church Street. My mother did the housework and cookin' and things like that 'til she was sold in the country.

I wish you could of talk to my mother. She know all 'bout slavery. She come from Nashville, Tennessee, and then to Texas. Her name was Mary Alexander. My father was name Matt Williams. Mr. Schwoebel own him. He use to belong to Mr. Sultry, befo' he sold him to Mr. Schwoebel for the day time, and [he] come back to his family at Mr. Sultry's at night. Lots of folks did that way when they was sold here.

Then we was sold to Tom Snow. No'm, we didn't go to no market to get sold. We got sold right here in Galveston without goin' no place else. You see they sold my mother, and me and my li'l brother had to go with her to the country. I think they sold her right at Mr. Sultry's. They never took 'er to no market, I know that. My father couldn't go with us. He wasn't sold to Mr. Snow, so he had to stay here. I ain't never seen him again. After the war, we come here to Galveston, but my father wasn't here.

Mr. Snow live in Polk County, two mile from Cold Springs. We was 'way out in the country. But we wasn't lonesome 'cause Mr. Snow had a big place. I can't tell you just how big it was 'cause I don't know, but he had a lot of field hands, and there was plenty for 'em to do. We live in the cabins. The white folks live in a wood house. Just a box house like this one, only lots bigger. It was white, I 'member that.

I can 'member the church, too. It was made out of wood, like the house, only it wasn't big. They had a white minister who use to come and have church 'bout every Sunday. The white folks went to church there, too. They sat in the front, and we sat in the back. Some of the old folks was funny. Some of 'em was old Christian people, and they couldn't do nothin' on Sunday. They couldn't even cook nor make a fire in the stove. We wasn't like that.

I never did no work. My mother was the cook for the white people, and my li'l brother, Charlie Evans, was a water toter in the field. Don't you know what that is? He bring a bucket of water 'bout the fields and give the hands a drink. Just a water boy, I guess you call it. That was all he did, but it kept him busy in the hot weather.

Plenty of times people run 'way out of the fields. They use to work awful hard, and the sun was awful hot, so they just run 'way. The only place they could go to was the woods, and they use to hide there.

Mr. Snow use to keep nigger dogs to hunt 'em with. They was the kind of dogs that has the big ears. I don't know 'bout 'em. They was so bad I never fool 'round 'em. Mr. Snow used to keep 'em chained up 'til one of the field hands run 'way. Then he turn 'em loose to get the scent. They kep' on 'til they found him, and sometimes they hurt him. I 'member hearin' them talk 'bout how they tore the meat off one of the field hands when they found him. I was 'fraid of 'em. I never went 'round 'em even when they was chained.

Mr. Snow use to whip the fields hands when they caught 'em from runnin' 'way. I never seen no whippin's, and I don't want to. But mostly they was 'fraid of the dogs.

I hear some of 'em say somethin' 'bout jumpin' over the broom and bein' married that way, but it ain't true. No'm, that's just a story. I seen a lot of marriages, and they was married regular. They use to call you in the church, and say matrimony over you, and call you man and wife. The minister married you just like the white folks. Some of the field hands didn't get married. They just live together without bein' married. Then when they got tired of the woman, they quit and go on 'bout their business. But don't you believe that story 'bout the broom, 'cause it ain't so.

We didn' have no schools. My mother couldn't read or write, and I can't neither. After slavery some of the ladies I work for learn me to say my ABCs but that's all.

My mother used to send me and my brother out in the woods to get her some of the blackberry roots. She use to make medicine out of 'em. She use to take it and boil it, then take it and strain it and give it to you for the worms. You just take a few drops at one time. I guess I 'member that 'cause I use to take so much of it.

Then she use to take the cornmeal and brown it in a pan 'til it was real brown and then make coffee out of it.

I don't 'member much 'bout the war. I didn't care much 'bout it 'til Mr. Snow told my mother we was free. We was all free, all the field hands and all. We didn't make no celebration over it. Me and my mother went here to Galveston as soon as we could, and my mother got work cookin', and I went with her.

John Walton

John Walton, age eighty-seven, was born August 15, 1849, a slave of Bill Walton who lived in Austin, Texas, until the Civil War. He then purchased a farm in Robertson County, Texas. John and his wife, Missouri, own a little home at 1008 Juniper Street, Austin. Each receives an old-age pension of ten dollars a month.

My name is John Walton, yes, sir, and I's born right here in Austin That on the fifteenth day of August 1849. I done had the papers on that, but where they is now I don't know. Pappy's named Gordon Walton, and I 'member he die while the war goin' on, or just befo'. My mammy was a small woman named Mary.

Massa Bill Walton owns all us. He the brother of Buck Walton, and us live in Austin 'til it said the Yankees comin'. Some Southern folks here in Austin was diggin' ground for a fort, old Fort MacGruder, just south of Austin. So Massa Bill takes us all 'way from Austin and up to Roberton County, 'cause he done figured the Yankees can't git up there.

I done field work up there, and even us kids had to pick

150 pounds cotton a day, or git the whuppin'. Us puts the cotton in the white-oak baskets, and some them hold more'n a hundred pounds. It 'cordin' to the way you stamps the cotton in. The wagon with yoke of oxen standin' in the field for to pour the cotton in. When it full, the oxen pulls that wagon to the hoss-power gin. Us gen'rally use 'bout sixteen hundred pounds cotton to make the bale.

Purty soon after Massa Walton opens he farm, he die. Missus Walton then marries a Dr. Richardson, and he git the overseer what purty rough on us. He want all us to stay right in line and chop 'long and keep up with the lead man. If us didn't, it am the bullwhip. He ride up and down and hit us over the back if us don't do the job right. Sometimes he'd git off he hoss, and have two slaves hold one down, and give him the bullwhip. He'd give it to him, too.

I helped break up the land, and plant and chop cotton, and a little of ever'thing. Just what had to be done at the time, I goes out and does it. I run 'cross plenty snakes, and one day one bit me right top the foot. There plenty varmints, too.

In the fall of the year us kill plenty hawgs and put the gamblin' racks [gambrel racks] and hang that meat up for the night. There some big dogs what watched the meat, and one old dog, old Jefferson, was bigger'n than any dog I ever seed. He kilt many 'nother dog. One night a big panther try steal the hawg meat, and old Jeff cotch him and helt him 'til the men comes. The panther tore Jeff up purty bad. Us heard them panthers scream at night, and if you didn't know, you'd think it were a woman. I could tell the diff'rence, 'cause the panther scream have the little growl at the end. If he half mile 'way, you'd hear that little whang.

One night I goes out in the bottom with my dog. I was huntin', but I don't like what I finds. A big panther follows me and old Nig—that my big, black bulldog. Scairt him 'way from me. I sho' run that night, and I never skip 'way no more at night.

Massa's big house set 'way from our cabins. Us have the big room where the slaves meals all cook. The fireplace 'bout four foot 'cross and plenty ashes in the mornin' to make the ashcakes. For breakfast us have meat and ashcakes and bran coffee or sassafras tea. You could keep them dried sassafras roots the year 'round, and they just as strong as coffee. Us plowed 'em up in the field, 'cause they grow wild.

Us didn't have time for the playin' of games durin' the week, 'cause it dark when us goes out, and it dark when us comes back. Us sho' was tired. At night that overseer walk by our cabins and call out to us, to see if us all inside. If us don't answer, he come up and find out why, and he'd find us, too.

I learned to read and write a little, just since Freedom. Us used Webster's old blue-black spellers. I has one in the house to this day, and I wouldn't take nothing for it.

The first year after Freedom, I farms with Mammy and my stepdaddy. Pappy done die. Us done purty good the first year, and I keeps on farmin' most my life. I marries Georgia Anne Harper in 1875 or 1876 in Limestone County. Us have four chillen, and three is livin'. I marries 'gain in 1882, to Missouri Fisher, and us have eight chillen and six is livin'. Us gits 'long on what the state give us now, and it ain't so bad. Times is diff'rent. I never done much but farm, so I don't know so much 'bout ever'thing what goes on.

Andy J. Anderson

Andy J. Anderson, age ninety-four, was born a slave to Mr. Jack Haley, who also owned Andy's parents with twelve other families and a plantation located in Williamson County, Texas. In view of the fact that all slaves used the name of their owner, Andy was known as Andy Haley, but after his freedom, he changed his name to Anderson, the name his father used, because he was owned by a Mr. Anderson before his sale to Mr. Haley. Shortly after the Civil War began, Andy was sold to Mr. W.T. House of Blanco County, Texas, who sold him again in less than a year to his brother, Mr. John House. After the Emancipation Act became effective, Andy was hired by a Mr. Whisterman. His first wages were his clothes, room and board, with two dollars per month. He farmed all of his life and has been married three times, now living with his third wife and eight of his children at 301 Armour Street, Fort Worth, Texas.

My name am Andy J. Anderson, and I's born on Marster Jack Haley's plantation in Williamson County, Texas. Marster Haley owned my folks and 'bout twelve udder fam'lies of cullud folks.

How come I's took the name of Anderson, 'stead of Haley? It am this-a way, my pappy was owned by Marster Anderson, who sold him to Marster Haley, so he goes by the name of Anderson. They use to call me Haley, but aftah Surrendah, I's change the name to Anderson to have it the same as my pappy's.

I's bo'n in 1843. That makes me ninety-four years old, and eighteen years old when the war stahted. Tharfo', this nigger has seen a good deal of slave life and some hahd 'speriences [experiences] durin' that time, and good times, too.

Marster Haley am kind to his cullud folks. In fact, him am kind to ever'body, and all the folks like him. Whuppin's am not given 'cept when it am necessary, and that am not often, and am reasonable when it am given. The udder white folks use to call we'uns the petted niggers.

The plantation have twelve fam'lies of slaves. Thar am 'bout thirty old and young workers and 'bout twenty pickaninnies that am too young fo' work. Them that am too young fo' work am took care of by a nurse durin' the day, while the mammies am a-workin' in the field and such.

I's gwine to 'splain how it am managed on Marster Haley's place. Marster Haley am a good manager, and ever'one am 'signed [assigned] to do certain jobs. It am diff'ent now than 'twas then. A plantation am sort of like the small town. Ever'thing that am used on the place am made thar. So, thar am the shoemaker. Him also am the tanner and make the leathah from the hides.

Thar am 'bout 1,000 sheep on the marster's place, so thar am the person that tends to the sheep and the wool. The sheep am sheared twice a yeah [year].

The wool am carded, spun, and weaved into cloth, and from that cloth, all the clothes am made. Thar am 'bout twenty-five head of cattle, such provides the milk and buttah, also beef meat fo' eatin'. Then thar am turkey, chickens, hawgs, and bees.

The plantation am planted in cotton, mos'ly. 'Co'se [of course], there am corn and wheat. The corn am fo' feed, and fo' the stock, and to make cornmeal fo' the humans. The wheat am fo' to make flour. Marster don't sell any corn or wheat, 'less if he have extra. Cotton am what he raised fo' sale.

Let me tell you's how we cut and thresh the wheat. Thar am no binders, or threshin' machines, so we'uns cut the wheat by hand, usin' a cradle. To thresh the grain, it am hung over a rail with the heads down, and the heads am beat with a stick. That knocks the kernels out, and they falls on a canvas that am spread to catch them. Now, to clean the wheat, we'uns have to wait fo' a day when the wind am blowin' just right. When that day comes, we'uns pick the wheat up with pails, raise it up, and pour it out, and the wind blows the chaff and sich away.

The livin' fo' the cullud folks am good. The quatahs [quarters] am build from logs like they's all am in them days. The floor am dirt, but we'uns have a table and bench, a bunk with straw ticks on fo' sleepin' pu'pose, and a fireplace fo' cookin' and heat. Marster 'lows plenty of good rations, but he watch close fo' the wastin' of the food.

The war starts, and that makes a big change on the marster's place. The marster joins the army and hires a man named Delbridge fo' overseer to help the marster's son, John. Then, in 'bout three months, the soldiers come and took Marster John to the army by force. They's put him on a hoss and tooks him away.

Thar come pretty near bein' some hurt niggers the day they's took Marster John away. You see, we'uns don' know they had the right to took marster away, so we'uns cullud folks crowded 'roun' the marster and warn't gwine to 'low them to took him. The marster told we'uns to go 'way 'cause the soldiers have the right to took him, and we'uns just git hurt if we'uns try to stop the soldiers, so we'uns dispatched.

After Marster John am took away, and the overseer am left in whole charge, hell stahts to pop. The first thing he does am to cut the rations. He weigh out the meat, three pounds to the person fo' the week, and he measures out a peck of meal, 'twarn't 'nough. He half starve the niggers and demands mo' work, and he start the whuppin's. I's guess he 'cides to edumacate [educate] them. I's guess Delbridge went to hell when he died . . . I's don't think he go that far, though. I's don't see how the devil could stand him.

We'uns cullud folks on marster's place am not used to such treatment and some run off. When they's am catched, thar am a whuppin' at the stake. Thar am a couple of the runaway niggers that am never catched.

I's 'scaped the worst of Delbridge, 'cause he sold me. I's sold to Marster W.T. House of Blanco County. I's sho glad when I's sold, but it am short gladness. I's not on that place long, just a few months 'til I's sold to his brother, John House, who had a big plantation close by.

I's git one whuppin' while on the W.T. House place. The scars am on my arms, see thar, and on my back, too. Them I's will carry to my grave. The whuppin' I's git am fo' the cause as I's will 'splain [explain]. 'Twas this a way. The overseer sent me fo' the dry fire wood. When I's gits the wood loaded and starts to drive, the wheel hits a short stump, the team jerks and that breaks the whippletree [a pivoted crossbar to which the traces of a harness are fastened]. I's tries to fix that so that the load could be hauled in. I's delayed quite a spell while the cook am waitin' fo' the wood. After I's tries and tries, it am necessary fo' me to walk to the barn fo' another whippletree. The overseer am at the barn when I's gits there. He am gittin' ready to start after me. I's tell what am the delay. He am pow'ful mad, 'cause I's hit the stump and sich.

The overseer ties me to the stake and ever half hour, fo' four hours, they's lay ten lashes on my back. Fo' the first couple of hours the pain am awful. I's never fo'git it. After I's stood that fo' a couple of hours, I's could not feel the pain so much. When they took me loose, I's just half dead. I's could not feel the lash, 'cause my body am numb, and my mind am numb. The last thing I's 'membahs am that I's wishin' for death. I's laid in the bunk fo' two days gittin' over that whuppin'. That is, gittin' over it in the body but not in the heart. No, sir! I's have that in my heart 'til this day.

After that whuppin', I's don't have my heart in the work fo' the marster. If I's see some cattle in the cornfield, I's turn my back 'stead of chasin' them out. I's guess the marster see that I's not to be depended on, and that's maybe the reason he sold me to his brother John.

John House am just the udder way from his brother 'bout the treatment of the cullud folks. Marster John never hit a nigger.

When Surrender am 'nounced, Marster right away tells his niggers that they am free. He calls all us together and tells we'uns that it am just a short time 'til the order fo' to free the niggers will be given. He says, "Now, them who stays will be paid wages, or we'uns shall 'range fo' workin' the land on shares." Where he am a-talkin' am in the field under a big tree. I's standin' near him, and there's where my big mouth gits me all fustup.

The marster finished his statement a-sayin', "All you's niggers can stay with me." I's says to myse'f, not loud 'nough fo' anyone to hear, I's thinks, but the marster hears me when I says, "Like hell I's will."

Now I's don't mean anythin' 'gainst the marster. What I's mean am that I's gwine to take my freedom, but he took it to mean something else. Somethin' 'gainst him, and he says:

"What is that you says, nigger?"

"Nothin', nothin' marster," I says.

"I's hears you, and I's will 'tend to you later," he says.

When that took place, it am 'bout one hour by sun. I's 'gain talkin' to myse'f, but I's sho keeps my lips closed. I's says, "I's won't be here long."

I's not realize what I's am in fo' 'til after I's started, but 'course I's couldn't turn back. Fo' to turn back maybe mean a whuppin' and to go on means danger from the patterollers. There I's was, but I's kep' on gwine. The patterollers' duties am to watch fo' the nigger that am without the pass. No nigger am 'posed to be off his marster's place 'less he have the statement from him. If the patters catch me, they's would give me a whuppin' and took me back to the marster. Well, him am already mad over what I's says, and I's 'spected [expected] a whuppin' there, so this nigger am in a perdicklement [predicament].

I's travel at night, and ever'time I's see someone a-comin', this nigger sho' hide 'til they's pass out of the way. In the day, I's keeps hidden in the brush with no water 'cept when I's come to a creek. I's sho' gittin' weak and tired the second night. Twice I's sho' the patters pass while I's hidin'.

I's then twenty-one years old, but it am the first time that I's go any place, 'cept to the neighbors, so I's worried 'bout the right way to Marster Haley's place. However, the mornin' of the third day, I's come to the marster's place, tired, hungry and skert 'bout the overseer 'cause Marster Haley am not home from the army yet. I's sho' wants to keep away from Delbridge, so I's waits my chance to see Pappy. When I's did, he sho' am s'prised to see me. Then I's told him what I's done, and he hides me in his cabin. There I's stay fo' a week, then luck comes to me when Marster Haley comes home.

The marster came home at night. The next mornin' befo' noon, Delbridge am shunt off the place. When the marster gits up in the mornin', he looks at the niggers. Lots have run off and the fields am not properly plowed. There am 'bout half of his sheep left, and the same with ever'thing.

The marster called Delbridge, and soon after, Hell am a-poppin'. The marster says to him, "Where is my sheep, chickens, hawgs, and all the udder stuff? What about them ga'nt [gaunt] niggers, and what did you's do with the rations?" Delbridge starts to talk and the marster says befo' he could say a word, "Shut up! There am no words can 'splain what you's done. Git off my place befo' I's smash you's!" Then 'twarnt long 'til Delbridge am gwine down the road with his bundle.

I's stay wid Marster Haley 'til Freedom am ordered. Then I's hired out to Marster Whisterman fo' two dollars a month with the clothes and board. The work was farm work. All my life, I's follow farm work.

I's married the first time in 1883. We'uns had two chilluns, but they both died. Then in 1885, I's married again. My second wife died in 1934. If she lived 15 days longer, we'uns would have been together 50 years. There was six chilluns born to we'uns. Three am livin' here and one in Belton, the udders am dead. I's married my present wife on June 11, 1936. There am no chilluns yet from my third marriage.

The last few years, I's not farmed but worked at odd jobs and raise chickens on this big lot I's live on. There am not much mo' work fo' this person. Still, I's healthy and able to work, but the Bible says four score and ten, and I's gittin' there.

Betty Farrow

Betty Farrow, age ninety, now living with a son on a farm in Moser Valley, a Negro settlement ten miles northeast of Fort Worth on Texas Highway #15, was born a slave to Mr. Alex Clark, plantation owner in Patrick County, Virginia, at that time. Betty is addressed as "Mammy Farrow."

I's glad to tells what I's know, but you's have to 'scuse me 'cause my 'collection [recollection] am bad. I's just don't 'member much. I'n bo'n on Marster Alex Clark's plantation in Patrick County, Virginny, June 28, 1847. That's what my mammy told me. You see, we'uns cullud folks have no schoolin' them days. I's can't read nor write. I's have to depends on what folks tells me.

Marster Clark had right-smart plantation in ol' Virginny. He owns 'bout twenty other slaves that wo'ked that big place. He had three girls and four boys. When I's a chile, we'uns used to play togedder. We'uns was 'tached to each udder all our lives.

In my mammy's fam'ly, there was five boys and four girls. I's

Betty Farrow
REPRODUCED FROM THE COLLECTIONS OF THE LIBRARY OF CONGRESS, LC-USZ62-125345

don't 'member 'bout my pappy. I's 'collects Mammy talkin' 'bout him some. When I's 'bout ten, I's was set to wo'k 'roun' the house. As I's gits older, they gives me mo' wo'k to does. I's always used mos'ly fo' housewo'k.

'Twas 'bout three yeahs befo' the war that Marster sold his plantation fo' to gwine to Texas. He keeps all the slaves and takes them with him. I's 'members the day we'uns started in three covered waggins, all loaded. The marster's wife, she cries pow'ful hard 'cause we'uns leavin' the ol' home. We'uns chilluns was a-havin' a good time, 'twas celebration day fo' us. We'uns travels from daylight to dark, 'cept to feed and rest the mules at noon. I's 'collects comin' over the mountains. Lawd, we'uns was skeert some of the time. Some times the marster's wife and the girls screetched, 'cause we'uns could look down, down, and down. If the wagon tips over, whar we'uns go? But, thank the Lawd, we'uns never tips over. I's can't 'collects how long we'uns was on the way, but 'twas a long time and 'twarn't a celeb'ation towards the last. After 'while when we'uns comes to Sherman, Texas, the marster stops on a farm.

When we'uns was at Sherman 'bout a year, there am heaps of trouble. There was a neighbor, Shields, he use to haul wood to town and drives 'cross Marster's yard. The marster and hims have arguments 'bout that. One day, we'uns chilluns was a-playin' back of the house. Marster was a-settin' on the front porch, and Shields was a-comin' up the road with the load of wood, gwine to town. Marster stops Shields when him starts 'cross the yard. The road had been there long times, but the marster wants to change it. Marster and Shields was a-talkin' loud. We'uns peaks 'round the side of the house, young chillens like, to see what's a-doin'. The first thing we knows, we'uns heard "Bang!" That man, Shields, shoots the marster, and we'uns sees the marster fall. Then Shields say "Giddap" to the mules and drives on like nothin's happened.

We'uns was skeert plum to 'straction [distraction] and runs in the house. We'uns hid behind the stove. Marster's wife and the girls goes a-runnin' to the marster, picks him up, and carries him in the house. They sends young Alex fo' the doctor mans. He rides a mule, and he makes that mule run like he never runs befo'. We'uns was all a-cryin' and moanin'. The girls was a-washin' the marster's face with water and rubbin' his hands. 'Twarn't long 'til the doctor mans comes drivin' in a buggy, and the hoss was a-runnin' like lightnin'. He comes in the house and looks at the marster, listens to his heart and sez, "He am dead." There was pow'ful sorrow in that home. 'Twas a long time befo' Mamma Clark was able to be herself.

After that, the marster's boy, Alex, take charge. Him and his mamma runs the farm. One day, 'bout a year after the shootin', Marster Alex sez to us, "We'uns have sold the land and am gwine to Fort Worth." We'uns packed the wagons again, and drove to Village Creek. That's 'bout ten miles east of Fort Worth. There, they settles on a farm, and we'uns all works hard, 'cause we'uns wants to git on for Mamma Clark and the boys.

If I's 'collects right, the war started the year we'uns moved to Village Creek. Two of the boys join the army. Durin' the war, we'uns all wo'ked hard and 'cepted what Mamma Clark had fo' us, 'cause she told us when the war started, "Now, the country is in heaps of trouble, and we'uns must help the best we'uns can, and not complain." There was times when there was not 'nough materials to make the clothes. You know, we'uns made all our clothes them times. We'uns always had plenty of things to eat, but some times they had to supply the army mans and that makes us short of some things.

When the war was over, the boys comes home, lookin' as pert as befo' they goes. We'uns stayed on workin'. I's don't 'member bein' told I's free. They might have told my mammy. I's don't see no diff'ence, we'uns just stayed. 'Twas our home, and they was good to us, 'twarnt any reason to leave. Mamma Clark died some years after the war. I's just can't 'member when, but we'uns all stays on with the boys, and keeps raisin' the corn and the wheat. My mammy stays with the Clark family all of her life.

I's get married when I's twenty-seven, then I's left the white folks' place. My husband rents a piece of land. We'uns farmed that fo' some years, then we'uns bought a farm here in Moser Valley. We'uns have farmed all our lives and cared fo' our chilluns. We'uns had ten chilluns, and it takes lots of things to care fo' that many. Sometimes we'uns had to skimp, but we'uns gets on. The oldest chile is sixty-two, and I's livin' with him now. When my husband died fifteen years ago, I's comes here and have been here ever since. I's never been in trouble. I's always too busy tendin' to my 'sponsibilities fo' to get in the devilment, and now I's happy tendin' to my great grandchile.

Adline Marshall

Adline Marshall, living at 3514 Bastrop Street, Houston, Texas, was born a slave somewhere in South Carolina. She was taken from her parents when bought by a Captain Brevard and brought to Texas while still a baby. She remembers nothing about her mother or father, and has no record of her age, saying that Captain Brevard told her she was a "South Ca'lina nigger" but never how he got her or who her parents were. Although suffering physically from her "miseries," Adline Marshall's mind is quite good, but the treatment slaves received has made her very resentful of slave owners in general, and her master in particular.

Yes, suh, Adline Marshall is my name all right, but the folks 'round here just calls me Grandma.

Lord have mercy, white folks, I's been here in this land too long. Yes, suh, too long, and I just ain't no 'count no more for nothing. I's got miseries in my bones, and just look at what I's got on my feet—just rags, that's all, rags. Can't wear nothing else on 'em 'cause they hurts so. That's what the red russet shoes what we wears in slave times do—just pizen [poison] the feet.

Yes, suh, I's telling you the truth.

Lord, Lord, that sure was bad times. Black folks just raised up like cattle in a stable, yes, suh. Only Cap'n Brevard, he what owned me, treat the hosses and cattle better'n he do the niggers.

Don't know nothing 'bout myself, 'cept on the cap'n's place down on Oyster Creek. He has the plantation 'twixt [between] the Bordens' and the Thatchers' plantations, and that's the only place I knows 'bout 'til I's freedomed. He says I's a South Ca'lina nigger what he bought back there and brung me with him here to Texas when I was just a baby. I reckon it's the truth 'cause I never knowed no mamma or no papa neither one. Yes, suh, this old nigger's had a hard time, Lord yes, 'cause from far back I can think, I's worked.

The old cap'n's a hard man, and the drivers was hard, too—all the time whipping and stropping the niggers to make 'em work harder. Didn't make no diff'rence to the c'ap'n how little you is—you goes out to the field 'most soon as you can walk. The drivers don't use the bullwhip on the little niggers, but they play switch on us what sting the hide plenty. Sometimes they puts a nigger in stocks and leave 'em there for two or three days — don't give 'em nothing to eat or a drink of water, just leave 'em 'til they're most dead. And does they die, just put 'em in a box and dig a hole out back of the horse lot, and dump 'em in and cover 'em up. Ain't no preaching service nor nothing, the poor nigger is just outen his misery, that's all.

Yes, suh, what I tells is the truth, 'cause I's in the fear of God, and I ain't going to do no lying for no one, no, suh. Old Cap'n was just hard on his niggers. I 'member the time they strops Old Beans what's so old he can't work good no more, and in the morning they finds him hanging from a tree back of the quarters—he'd hung hisself to 'scape his misery.

We works every day 'cept Sundays, and we has to do our

washing then. Does anyone get sick during weekdays and can't work for mebbe two days, they has to work Sundays to make it up. And when we comes in at night, we has to go right to bed. They don't 'low us to have no light in the quarters, and you better be in bed and not sitting 'round after work if you don't want to get a whipping.

All we gets to wear is just a plain cotton slip with a string 'round the neck, just the same kind of stuff what they make the picking sacks of. Don't make no diff'rence if it winter or summer, that's all we get to wear.

Old Cap'n has a big house, but I just see it from the quarters, 'cause we wasn't 'lowed to go up in the yard. I hear 'em say he don't have no wife but has a black woman what stays at the house. That's the reason why there is so many "no nation" niggers 'round now. Some call 'em "bright" niggers, but I calls 'em no nation niggers, 'cause that's what they is—they ain't all black, and they ain't white, but they is mixed. That comes from slave times and the white folks did the wrong, 'cause the blacks get beat and whipped if they don't do what the white folks tell 'em to.

Lord have mercy, white folks sure did everything to the poor niggers 'fore we was freedomed. Work us early, work us late. Don't 'low us to visit none on other plantations, and just feed us cornbread and side meat. I never know nothing 'bout no church meetings or nothing outside cap'n's cotton field 'til I was freedomed. No, suh, I's tell you the truth.

I knows I's good size when Old Cap'n calls us in from chopping and tells us we's free, but nobody told me how old I was, and I never find out.

I knows some of us stays and works for something to eat, 'cause we didn't know no one and didn't have nowhere to go.

Then one day, Capn' come out in the field with 'nother man,

and pick me and four more what was working and tell the man we is good workers. That was Mr. Jack Adams what had a place down by Stafford's Run. He says if we want to work on his place, he feed us and give us good quarters and pay us for working, and that's how come I leaves Old Cap'n', and I ain't never see him or the place where I was raised up since, but I reckon 'cause he was so mean, the debbil's [devil] got him in torment long time ago.

I works in the field for Mr. Jack, and that's where Wes Marshall, what I married, worked, too. After we gets married, we gets us a piece of ground from Mr. Jack, and we stays on the same place 'til Mr. Jack die and we come to Houston. That was 'fore the 1900 storm.

I tell you what else is the truth. I tells when the storm is coming, yes, suh, that's gospel truth. And I ain't believe in no witch doings, but God tells me when a storm is coming.

I tell folks when the 1900 storm is coming, and they laugh at this old nigger. But it comes, and they loses horses, and cattle, and chickens, and sometimes the storm blows away, but it don't hurt a feather on my chickens, no, suh, 'cause the good Lord known I's telling folks the truth, and he pertects me.

Yes, suh, white folks, I's tell you the truth just like it is—I's had a hard time in the land. Why in this sinful town, they don't do like the Good Book say to do. No, suh, they don't. It say, "love thy neighbor," but folks don't love nobody but themselves.

Just look at me. I's old with misery, and I's all alone in the world. My husband and all my chillen die long ago and leave me here, and I just go from house to house to try to find a place to stay. That's why I's praying to God to take me to his bosom, 'cause He's the onliest one I got to call on.

Calvin Moye

Calvin Moye was born in 1842 in Atlanta, Georgia. When he was somewhere between eight and ten years old, the Ingram family moved to Rural Shade, Texas, where Mr. Ingram purchased a five- to six-hundred-acre ranch.

I was born in Atlanta, Georgia, December 25, 1842. My father and mother's boss told them to calls me Calvin, so that was what they named me—Calvin Moye.

My father's name was Isom, and my mother's name was Mamie Moye. Both of them was born and brought up there by Masser Richmond Ingram's father and later moved to Atlanta, Georgia, when they was about grown. Of course, they married like we do now, but they was married anyway as far as Masser Ingram was concerned, and they was bound to each other as much as we is now. Some plantations didn't see it that way, but Masser Ingram did.

My mother and father had seven chilluns, and they raised us all to be grown under the same masser. I has two brothers older than me. Louis was the oldest, and Aaron was the next. I had four sisters—Delia, Adalyn, and Mary. The other died when small. We were all born in Georgia and was on a plantation a little way from Atlanta. It was owned by Masser Ingram's father and handed down to him and another brother when he died, but they didn't agrees with each other, so when I was a big boy, maybe eight or ten years old, Masser Ingram traded his part to his brother, and we all hits out to Texas. He knew a man out here somewhere, so he writes Masser Ingram about this rich country. Masser Ingram sells out, and gets some ox wagons fixed up, and buys a lots of food, and puts in all we can that we has at the plantation, and starts out with seventy slaves that is big enough to work and their chilluns. We started once to comes to Texas coast by boat, but he decided we could come by ox wagons, so we start out. Sometimes we would comes to creeks and rivers that we couldn't cross, and we could travel up or down the stream huntin' a place to cross, and maybe we couldn't find one, so we would either build a pole bridge or put light logs on the side of the wagons and float them across like boats. We would do this if the stream was very wide, but if it was narrow and deep we would build a pole bridge and sometimes we would has to cut a road up and down the stream, but we were all comin' to Texas, a new country, and we didn't care. We was seein' new things every day. If the stream was very big, we would find a ferry. We crossed the Mississippi and Arkansas River, or Red River, I don't know which, on a ferryboat. Anyway, I remembers was two big rivers we crossed, and we would camp in the night and travel in the daytime. Every evening before camp time some of the older men would travel along ahead of us, out to the side of the road, and kill fresh meat for us to eat, or if we came to a river or creek, we would stop long enough for the menfolks to takes a seine and catch some fish.

There was always plenty to eat for us when we comes to

Texas. Sometimes when we camped in the river bottoms, we could hear the panthers scream and varmints of all kinds, but Masser Ingram always had some of the men stay up all night and watch out for the stock and the rest of us. We always camped close to water, so we could has plenty of water for us and the stock. Them ole oxen would runs to water when they begins to gits thirsty, and they would drag wagon and all right out in the middle of a water hole if they was pretty thirsty and had been drove pretty hard. You just couldn't hold them back, and they cans smells water a long ways. If we happened to comes for a long ways and not run across any water, we could always tell when we was gettin' close to water by the way them oxens acted. They was slow, but they would gits in a hurry when they was thirsty and was smellin' water.

When we comes to these streams and floats the wagons across, we would swim the stock across. Masser Ingram rode a hoss, and when we comes to a warm stream, he would let me hold his hoss's tail and swim across, and when we was out on the road, I would hold his hoss's tail and run along behind him while the hoss was trottin'. Sometimes he would kick the hoss in a long fast pace and stand me on my head in the dirt.

We had several dogs that belonged to some of the slaves that Masser Ingram lets them bring along. My father had one, and they helps to watch at night. The men that watched at night slept in the wagons in the daytime when we was all travelin'. When we camped for the night, we would pulls all the wagons in a big circle and puts the tongue of one wagon under the back end of another, and puts the stock in this circle and turns them loose. At first we couldn't sleeps for them and the varmints hollerin', but we finally got use to them and got to where we could sleeps as sound as we could back in Georgia in our log cabins.

We didn't has no trouble gittin' plenty of meat and fish for us to eat, but we had trouble gittin' feed for the stock. We grazed them along quite a bit, but grass-fed stock don't last very long when they is drove hard. They is like people that don't has much to eat, they gits tired and gives out quick. They needs lots grain to makes them strong, and when we couldn't git grain to feed them, we would drives them slow and grass them quite a bit. Grass was good, and the further west we got, the better the grass was and the harder the grain was to git to feed our stock.

Creeks and rivers back in them days did not overflow like they does now. The hills hadn't been plowed up and washed down in the bottom of the streams and half-way filled 'em up, and they gits the water quicker then they do now. The creeks and rivers was deeper, and the banks was steeper then they is now. People didn't use to know what had gone wrong if they had over-flows every year and washed the crops away.

When we first comes in here, the Trinity River and these creeks 'round here didn't overflow like they is now. We crossed Trinity River on a ferry, down where Wild Cat Ferry is now, when the river was up, and when it was down you could ford it. But these streams didn't dry up like they does now in the summer, they runs all the year 'round.

When we got to Navarro County, there warn't no railroads or nothin' much in the east end of the county. All that I knows of was Bazett, Chatfield, or Taos at Porto's Bluff, that is what they call it now. There ain't nothin' there now, but there use to be a little town there. It come might near bein' the state capital, but Austin beats them a little. Then there was a little town that grows up where we called Rural Shade, that is where Masser Ingram stops at and bought about five or six hundred acres of the levelest land that I ever saw. It was rich and had grass as high as my head on it, some of the best grazin' any of us had ever seen. There was plenty timber 'round everywhere, ain't like it is now, just timber 'round the riverbanks and creeks. There was timber most every-where. If a man wants fat stock it was his own fault that he didn't has them, 'cause the grass was here for everybody's stock to graze. There was plenty of nuts for the hogs to fatten on, and the people that was here had a good time them days, always something to goes to. They wasn't all in a hurry like they is now.

They gots to be lots of cowboys 'round here, and they would ride wild bronco horses and run races and has a good time. What people calls a good time now is gettin' half full of booze, and gettin' in a good car, and startin' out spendin' money, and just thinkin' they is havin' a good time.

But people in them days was different, they was most all friendly. 'Course we had them patterollers that was allus poppin' up and askin' for your pass, and they would whips you if you didn't have one. But we always had a pass, 'cause when we went anywhere, Masser Ingram always give us a pass, and we would show it when a white man asked us what we was doin'.

'Course there was whiskey in that time same as we has it now. People drinks it same as they does now, and they used it for sick folks more then they does now. But when people went out to picnics, and horse races, and public gatherings, they didn't half of them gits mightly drunk and tries to raise a racket with everybody they see, like they does now. If any man gits drunk, some men would takes him off and keeps him away 'til he sobers up.

When we first pulls in and camped, we was camped for three or four days before Masser Ingram found the land he wanted and gits it bought. Then he puts us all to cuttin' logs, buildin' rail fences, buildin' houses, barns, and other outbuildings. We all worked and were worked hard. The first house that was finished was Masser Ingram's, and the meat house, and the smokehouse, and barn. Then we went to buildin' houses for the slaves. My father was the first one to gits a house, and then one by one, the cabins was finished until we gits every family a big one-room log cabin built. Every house was covered with boards, instead of shingles like we has now, and they had very few nails in them. Then we builds a big blacksmith shop, opened to the south, and logs standin' straight up and down on the other three sides, and other furniture for all the slaves and Masser Ingram was made. All the blacksmith work was done, too, such as shapin' plows, makin' beams for plows, tongues for wagons, spokes, hubs, fellows for the wagon wheels, and everything that could be made to be used for the farm. All this was made out of oak that we got on the farm. As soon as the shed was finished, Masser Ingram says to me, "Now, Calvin, this is where I wants you to start to work. You begins in the mornin', so gits up and come down here ready to goes to work. Uncle Zeke is gettin' ole, and I's goin' to needs a new blacksmith before long, and you is the one I needs."

So the next mornin' I was down to the shop befo' Uncle Zeke was, 'cause I sho' was glad to gits out of that field work, and I knows I's would like that blacksmith work. Uncle Zeke starts me out to splittin' the oak logs. We splits out several, and then we starts to smoothin' out the boards, layin' each part in a separate place for the tables and the same way for the chairs each day 'til we gits enough made for everybody befo' we puts any of them together. Uncle Zeke watchin' and tellin' me all the time, and befo' we got through, he said I was about as good as he was.

We didn't has as much tools to work with as the cabinet-makers do now, but we made furniture that stood more rough treatment than the ones they makes now. We makes the straightback chairs with pegs for nails and rawhide bottoms, 'stead cane bottoms like we all buys now. The rawhide bottom didn't look as nice, but it lasted three or four times as long as the ones do now.

We made the highback rockin' chairs and made our own rockers, and made our own bedsteads and boards for slats, but we couldn't make no springs, we just puts the boards 'cross the rails, and puts our straw and grass mattresses on these boards, and sleeps just as good as anybody does on springs now, and gits just as much rest. The beds we made in slavery times could be took down and moved around just as easy as they can now. The boards and post was all just as smooth and good lookin' as any unpainted bedsteads now. Most of the bedsteads we made was big high ones. They was made about six feet high with big heavy posts, and we cuts different designs on the headboards and footboards and posts, and 'specially on the ones that we made for Masser Ingram. He drawed the designs on a paper, and brought them out to Uncle Zeke, and told him he wanted his made exactly like that. When we got through with them, they was the prettiest beds I's ever seen. He saw some like them back east somewhere that some rich people had, and they was expensive, but I bet they wasn't any stouter then the ones that Uncle Zeke and me made.

The log house that my mother and father lived in was a big one room with puncheon floors in it. A puncheon floor is a floor made of split logs and hewed down to fit together tight, and smoothin' the splits sides with a broad axe, and turnin' it up. It took men that knowed what they was doin' to make a floor out of this kind of timber, and makes it level, so you wouldn't has a table or a bed standin' on three legs or havin' little pockets in the floor. But all of Masser Ingram's houses had the same kind of floors in them, even his.

There was lots of good prairie grass in them days, but people didn't take care of it like they does now. They would graze the dead grass in the wintertime 'til somebody comes along and throws match in it and starts a big fire. I has seen lots of them prairie fires, and I has helped fight some of them. When a fire would git started with a good south wind, it would nearly outrun a horse. A man didn't have no chance at all. About the only way to stops one was for a big bunch of men to gits in ahead of it if the wind wasn't too high, and fire agins [against] it. That is, to starts a fire in the grass a good piece ahead of the big fire, and let the back side of the fire burn back to the big fire comin' on. But if the fire that we started was too slow in burnin' back to the big fire, sometimes the big fire would jump over all we burned over in the grass behind us, and there was plenty of trouble on our hands. The smoke would be so bad that we couldn't see another man thirty feet away unless we got down on the ground. Most of the time the grass was so tall you couldn't see them then. Just make you feel like you was fightin' that big fire yourself.

When one of them fires gits started I has seen the smoke goin' to the clouds and burnin' grass flyin' high in the air, and flames leapin' fifty feet in the air comin' towards me, and that sho' looked scary. You could see rabbits runnin' everywhere. Even 'possums, rats, skunks, and hawks would fly around and around over the grass in front of the fire, and they would fly down in the grass in a little open place. Then we would see them come up with a rabbit or something else in their claws and fly away. After the fire would pass on, you could walk back over the burned grass and find skunks, 'possums, rats, and rabbits burned to death. Sometimes some of them would git in holes that was deep enough to keep them from burnin' or roastin', and the smoke maybe runs them out after the fire had passed on. They would run 'til their feet would be burned so bad they would falls over and kicks around 'til somebody kills them, or they die.

Ever' fall Masser Ingram would sends two wagons and four men to Grand Saline for salt. They would just piles the salt in the wagons loose, and it would take the two wagonloads for us all to cook with and salts down the meat. This would last us about a year, and when Masser Ingram would see that we was goin' to run low on salt the next year he would send a third wagon that fall, but that would be about every three or four years. That extra salt with the two wagonloads the next year would run us for a few years. Another job we had to do in late fall was to thrash our wheat and cleans it for our flour and coffee. The way we cuts the wheat was with a scythe or cradle. We would cradle the wheat, and let it dry out good, and then takes it to a log house with puncheon floors in it. We would take some tough limbs with lots good switches on it and whips and beats the straw and all 'til we would whips the wheat out of the heads. Then we would take up the straw and pile it up somewhere outside and takes all the wheat in baskets. We would sweep the floor, and when the wind was blowin' good we would wind it—that is to pour the wheat from one basket to another holdin' the basket that you pours it out of about three or four feet above the one on the ground, and the wind would blow the chaff and dirt out of it.

We made our own flour on the plantation. It was all whole-wheat flour. It was awful dark and wasn't pretty and white like our flour is now. It was better than eatin' cornbread three times a day all the year. We used the wheat grains to make our coffee. We would puts it in a big three-legged iron skillet and put a cast-iron lid over it, and puts it over some hot ashes and coals, and parch it slow, and then grinds it up, and makes our coffee out of it.

All the boys growin' up had to learn how to do everything there was to do. Masser Ingram had the girls learn everything that a woman was supposed to know, so when she gots married they wouldn't has to fool around tryin' to learn how to do things.

The only thing that went against me in the blacksmith shop was I didn't knows how to figure and write. The white folks didn't tries to learn us anything 'long that line 'ceptin to count money, and he learns me how to do that. My father could read and write a little, but my mother didn't know how to do either one. I can reads now a little in the Bible, and I can write my name if I have plenty of time. Once and awhile when we was small chilluns my father would reads the Bible to us all, but he read slow like I does now.

Louise Mathews

Louise Mathews, 2718 Ennis Avenue, Fort Worth, Texas, was born a slave to a Baptist preacher, Reverend Robert Turner, who owned seven slave families, including Louise's mother and her nine children, on a small farm located near Bucksnort [since changed to Tenaha] in Shelby County, Texas. Louise knows nothing of her father. Jack Hooper, a neighboring farmer, owned her stepfather. She married Henry Daggett when she was twenty. Three children were born to them before his death in 1884. She married Jim Byers in 1885. One child was born to them. They were separated in 1886. She married Bill Mathews in 1887. Three children were born to them before his death on May 15, 1937. Four children are now dead.

Sho' I's 'membahs slavery times, 'cause I's eighty-three years old now. I's eleven years old when the breakup [Surrender] comes. I's bo'n in Shelby County, Texas, on the farm that belongs to Marster Robert Turner. Ever'body calls him Judge Turner. He was a Baptist preacher, and run a small farm and gen'ral store, too. Thar am seven fam'lies of slaves on Marster's place. 'Twas

Louise Mathews

my mother, she had nine chilluns, and six udder fam'lies. I's don't know nothin' 'bout my father, 'cept I's told he am in Virginia. When I's old 'nough to 'membahs, Mother am married to Tom Hooper. He am owned by Marster Jack Hooper, that owns a farm four miles from Marster's place. Marster Turner am the preacherman that married them.

Mostest the cullud folks just lives together by 'greement in slavery times, but 'twas diffe'nt on Marster's place. The marster says the ceremony fo' the marriage. He gits the couple together and says, "Do you's tooks this man to be you's husband, and do you's tooks this womens to be you's wifes? What the Lawd joins together, let no man put asunder." You's see, 'twas jus' like the white folks does when they marries.

We'uns lives in cabins built from logs. They am double cabins, and mostest of them have two fam'lies livin' in them. They am just like all udder cabins in slavery times, with dirt floor, no windows, just holes in the wall. We'uns sleeps in bunks with straw ticks. The cabins all had a fireplace, but they's used for heat, mostly in the wintertime. The cookin' am done at one place. 'Twas my gran'mammy that done the cookin' fo' the workers. Now, 'twas 'lowed to cook in the cabins for special doin's, like if there am a visitor. My mammy always cooks in her cabin when my stepfather comes to see we'uns. He comes ever' Wednesday and Saturday night, and then she cooks the meals fo' we'uns. Sho', Marster 'lows that, and my stepfather had a good marster, too.

I's gwine tell you's how my stepfather's marster does with most of his slaves. He 'lows them one acres of land and gives them time to work it. All they makes on the acre am given to the nigger. Father always plants his acre in cotton, and when Marster Hooper takes his cotton to town, Father's cotton goes, too. What it brings am given to Father. Well, that way, Father can buy things fo' himself so he has his own hoss and saddle, and he brings us good things to eat our marster don't furnish, such as the coffee and tea. Co'se, he brings us candy sometimes, and things to play with. 'Twas green coffee that Father always brings, and Mammy would roast, grind it, and make coffee fo' all us when her man comes to visit we'uns.

Marster Turner always gives we'uns good rations. That way, he am awful good, but what Father brings am just extra. Father sho' does well with his acre of land. Co'se he gets all his rations and clothes from his marster just like all slaves does, so he could save all he makes. Well, when Surrendah comes, he had over $500 saved, and 'twarn't worth a cent. I's 'membahs how he called all us chilluns together and says, "Here am lots of money you's can have." We'uns took it and plays store with it. 'Twas Confederate money am the reason 'twarn't no good.

We'uns sho' lives good on Marster Turner's place. Co'se, they raises ever'thing they uses in them days, and 'twas plenty of it. Lots of corn, cane, veg'tables, 'sides the cotton. 'Twas plenty of hawgs fo' the meat, cows fo' the milk and buttah, chicken fo' chicken meat and eggs, and bees fo' the honey. So, the rations am plenty of good food. No, sir, we'uns am never hungry. The clothes we'uns have am made on the marster's place on his own loom. We'uns always had plenty linsey-woolsey clothes.

Let me tell you's how the young'uns am cared fo'. They's given special care by the marster. The food am lots of clabber milk, cornbread, pot liquor wid cornbread crumbled up in it. 'Twas good food fo' sho' 'cause they's all fat and healthy. The marster had a special medicine fo' we'uns that he makes. You's see, he runs a store and sells whiskey.

Yas, sar, he am a preacherman, farmer, and a saloonkeeper. Well, now I's tells you's how he makes the medicine. He tooks some whiskey and puts cherry bark in it, also the rust off nails and iron. That am the medicine we'uns have to took. Well, it must be good 'cause 'twarn't much sickness, and we'uns am all fat and sassy. Gosh fo' mighty! How I's hates to took that medicine! Bittahs am what 'twas called, and 'twas bittah fo' sho'. The marster tends to givin' the bittahs himself. He am pa'ticular 'bout the young'uns, how they's fed and ever'thing. I's often hear him says to Anne, that am the cullud womens that tooks care of the chilluns, "Anne, tooks good care of the young'uns 'cause the old ones gwine to play out some time, and I's wants the young'uns to grow to be strong niggers."

'Twarn't no whuppin's that I's knows of. All the cullud folks am satisfied with what the marster gives them, and tries hard to please him, and he am satisfied with the workers, so 'twarn't no trouble.

'Twas only one runawayer, and he runs back to the marster's farm 'stead of 'way from him. 'Twas this way, Marster hires him out to a man named Murphy. Well, Murphy works the man all night and day, and then ain't satsified so the cullud fellow runs off and comes home. Sho', the marster often hires out a slave if they can spare one and some udder marster am short of help. The marster would hire one out fo' so much a day. Well, when John shows up at home, Marster asks him why he came home. John told him how he am worked, and Marster says he did him just right. He says, "I's don't hire you's out to be worked to death." That same day, Murphy shows up and wants to get John, but Marster says, "No, sir! I's knows John am a good worker, and when he says he am overwo'ked, I's knows he am overworked." Murphy am riled 'bout it but had to go off without John.

Marster Turner am very reasonable 'bout the work. He wants a good day's work, and all the cullud folks gives it to him. We'uns had Saturday afternoons off, and co'se, Sundays, too. We'uns does the washin' and such work as we'uns wants to do fo' ourselves on Saturdays, then we'uns could go to parties at night. The marster gives we'uns a pass ever' Saturday night if we'uns wanted it. We'uns had to have a pass 'cause the patterollers am watchin' fo' the cullud folks as don't have the pass. We'uns singin' and dancin' at the parties. The dancin' am quadrilles [a square dance for four couples] and the music am fiddles and banjoes.

We'uns all goes to chu'ch on Sundays. Co'se, the marster am the preacher. He preached to his white folks in the evenin'. 'Twas cullud folks as comes from all 'round udder plantations to we'uns chu'ch. That am the way we'uns lives on the marster's place, and 'twas the same on Stepfather's place.

Ever'thing am changed when Surrendah comes. Well does I's 'membahs the day Marster Turner come out in the yard of the cullud quartahs, and calls all us 'round him. I's can see him now, like I's watched him comin' to the yard with his hands clasped 'hind him and his head bowed, walkin' slowly. When he gets to the yard, he tells my uncle to call all us to him. When we'uns gets together, he starts talkin' slowly, and says, "Folks," I's 'membahs the words well, "I's likes ever' one of you's. You's have been faithful but I's have to give you's up. I's hates to do it, not 'cause I's don't want to free you's, but 'cause I's don't want to lose you's all. I's guess 'tis the bestest fo' you's, and fo' that, I's glad. You's from this moment am free folks just like I am, or the udder white folks." Then he stops talkin' fo' a little bit, and we'uns could see tears in his eyes. When he talks 'gain, he says, "I's wants you's all to stay on the farm, and we'uns can work the land on shares."

Most the cullud folks leaves the place and went back to the folks Marster buys them from. Some went to Dawg Robinson, some to Maddox, and some to Reeves. Co'se, my mammy tooks we'uns chilluns and goes to Hooper's place where Father am, and we'uns lives there on the Hooper Place fo' seven yeahs after the breakup. We'uns come to Fort Worth in 1872, and 'twas right where we'uns am livin' now. 'Twarn't settled then. We'uns farmed land where all the houses am now in this section.

Reason Father moves from Shelby County am 'cause the Ku Klux Klan gets so bad pesterin' the niggers the menfolks am 'fraid to sleep in the house, and would go to ravines, the woods, and such where they could hide. We'uns never had any trouble on Marster's place but am 'fraid to go any place. 'Twas two cullud men shot near we'uns. The Klux comes to the house, and the cullud fellows tries to fit [fight] them off. 'Cause the cullud fellows fits them, the Klux shoots them.

Father gets 'gusted [disgusted] after that and says, "'Tis time to move from such country." After we'uns come heah, I's gets married the first time. 'Twas in 1874, and I's twenty yeahs old. 'Twas to Henry Daggett. He belong to Marster Daggett befo' Surrendah, and he lives on the Daggett ranch. He dies in 1884. 'Bout a yeah after that, I's married to Jim Byers, and we'uns sep'rated the next yeah. That man was lazy and no 'count. I's just keeps fustin' with him, and 'sistin' [insisting] that he go to work. When he sees that I's means it, he leaves, and 'twas the last I's ever sees of him. 'Twas on a Christmas Day in the mornin', an 'twas the only Christmas present he ever made me. He am what am called the "buck passer." I's did washin' and ironin', and he passes the bucks I made away. I's marries Bill Mathews the next yeah. He makes we'uns' livin' at common labor but am 'dustrious [industrious] and tooks good care of his fam'ly.

I's the mother of seven chilluns. 'Twas three by Henry Daggett, one by Jim Byers, and three by Bill Mathews. He died on May 15, this yeah. Just one of my chilluns am still livin', and they's all here in Fort Worth.

Votin'? Well, I's only voted once 'bout four yeahs ago. I's just don't care 'bout it, 'cause 'tis too much fustin' 'round. Bill

Mathews always voted in the gen'ral 'lection, and he always voted the Lincoln ticket.

Yas, sir, my health am good. I's gets 'round and does my housework. I's feels good, but I's know 'twon't be long 'til I's goes to the restin' place the Lawd has fo' we'uns.

Wash Ingram

*Wash Ingram, age ninety-three, was born a slave of Captain Jim
Wall of Richmond, Virginia. His father, Charley Wall Ingram, ran
away and secured work in a gold mine. Later, his mother died, and
Captain Wall sold Wash and his two brothers to Jim Ingram of
Carthage, Texas. When Wash's father learned this, he overtook his
sons before they reached Texas and put himself back in bondage, so
he could be with his children. Wash served as water carrier for the
Confederate soldiers at the battle of Mansfield, Louisiana. He now
lives with friends on Elysian Fields Road, seven miles southeast of
Marshall, Texas.*

I don't know just how ole I is. I was 'bout eighteen when the
war was over. I was born on Captain Wall's place in Richmond,
Virginia. Pappy's name was Charlie and Mammy's name was
Caline. I had six sisters and two brothers, and all the sisters is
dead. I haven't heard from my brothers since Master turned us
loose, a year after the war.

Pappy say that he and Mammy was sold and traded lots of
times in Virginia. We always went by the name of whoever we

belonged to. I first worked as a roustabout boy there on Captain Wall's place in Virginia. He was sho' a big man, weighed more'n two hundred pounds. He owned a lot of niggers and worked lots of land. The white folks was good to us, but Pappy was a fightin' man, and he run off and got a job in a gold mine in Virginia.

After Pappy run away, Mammy died. Then one day, the overseer hurried up a big bunch of us niggers and drive us to Bernu'ms Tradin' Yard down in Mississippi. That's a place where they sold and traded niggers just like stock. I cried when Captain Wall sold me, 'cause that was one man that sho' was good to his niggers. But he had too many slaves.

Cotton was a good price then, and them slave buyers had plenty of money. We was sold to Jim Ingram of Carthage. He bought a big gang of slaves and refugeed part of 'em to Louisiana and part to Texas. We come to Texas in ox wagons. While we was on the way—camped at Keachie, Louisiana—a man come ridin' into camp, and someone say to me, "Wash, there's your pappy." I didn't believe it 'cause Pappy was workin' in a gold mine. Some of the men told Pappy his chillen is in camp, and he come be with his chillen.

Master Ingram had a big plantation down near Carthage and lots of niggers. He also buyed land, cleared it, and sold it. I plowed with oxen. We had a overseer and sev'ral taskmasters. They whip niggers for not workin' right, or for runnin' 'way, or pilferin' 'round Master's house. We woke up at four o'clock and worked from sunup to sundown. They give us an hour for dinner. Them that work 'round the house ate at tables with plates. Them that work in the field was drove in from work and fed just like hosses at a big, long wooden trough. They had to eat with wooden spoons. The trough and the food was clean and always plenty of it, and we stood up to eat. We went to bed soon after supper durin' the week for that's 'bout all we feel like doin' after workin' twelve hours. We slept in wooden beds what had corded rope mattresses.

We used to learn the best way we could, 'cause there was no schools. We had church out in the woods. I didn't see no money 'til after Surrender. Guess we didn't need any, 'cause they give us food, and clothes, and tobacco. We didn't have to buy nothin'. I had broadcloth clothes, a blue jean overcoat, and good shoes and boots.

Sat'day night we would have parties, and dance, and play ring plays. We had the parties there in a big double log house. They would give us whiskey, and wine, and cherry brandy, but there was no shootin' or gamblin'. They didn't 'low it. The men and women didn't do like they do now. If they had such carryin' on as they do now, the white folks would have whipped 'em good.

I 'member the war, and I sees them cannons and hears 'em. I toted water for the soldiers what fought at the Battle of Mansfield. Master Ingram had 350 slaves when the war was over, but he didn't turn us loose 'til a year after Surrender. He told us that the gov'ment goin' to give us forty acres of land and a pair of mules, but we didn't git nothin'. After Master Ingram turn us loose, Pappy bought a place at De Berry, Texas, and I live with him 'til after I was grown. Then I marry and move to Louisiana. I come back to Texas two years ago and live with my friends here ever since. My wife died eighteen years ago, and I had a hard time 'cause I don't have no folks, but I's managed to git someone to let me work for somethin' to eat, a few clothes, and a place to sleep.

Lucy Thomas

Lucy Thomas, a native Negress of Harrison County, was born in 1851, as a slave of Dr. William Baldwin. She left the Baldwins with her parents in 1868, moving to the Haggerty place. In 1869 she was married to Anthony Thomas, living with him fifty-five years and rearing seven children. Lucy continued to earn her own living on the farm after the death of her husband until about three years ago. At the present time she is living with her son at Baldwin Switch, sixteen miles northeast of Marshall on the Long's Camp Road. Her son is farming part of the land originally settled by the Baldwins. Lucy now receives a ten-dollar-per-month old-age government pension.

My name is Lucy Baldwin Thomas. I was bo'n here in Harrison County on the Dr. Baldwin place at Fern Lake. The log cabin where I was bo'n sat in a grove of trees right there by the lake. The Baldwin place jined [joined] the Haggerty, Fitzpatrick, Cavin and Major Andrews places. It set right in the middle of them.

The best statement I can make of my age is that I was 'bout

Lucy Thomas
REPRODUCED FROM THE COLLECTIONS OF THE LIBRARY OF CONGRESS, LC-USZ62-125309

fourteen the last year of Abe Lincoln's war. I 'members my mother saying we had been free four years when I married, and that I was eighteen years old when me and Anthony Thomas got wedded. I was big enough to chop cotton the first year of Abe Lincoln's war. You can figurate my age from that. I went to work in the field hoeing when I was nine years old and has worked in the field ever since 'til 'bout three years ago.

They called my father Ike. The Baldwins bought him out of Alabama. My mother's name was Nancy. She was bo'n in Virginia, but the Baldwins bought her out of the New Orleans slave market for eleven hundred dollars. The Baldwins brought my grandma, Barbara, to Texas with them. I's heard her tell how some of the owners in Alabama dug their darkies with a mule and laid them face down in a hole and beat them 'til them was raw as beefsteak. She say the darkies on lots of places had to hide out to sing and pray. Her folks warn't like that. She say she allus belonged to good white folks like the Baldwins. I had two brothers, Anthony, named for Mother's father, and Will Cammack, named for our daddy's first master. There was seven girls: Me, Floreda, and Rosetta was named for our mother's sisters; Barbara was named for Mother's mother; Pink and Lethe was named for friends; and Nancy was named for her mother.

My mistress was named May Amelia. She had five boys and three girls: Ben, Will, Lewis, Phil, and George, and Millie, Nannie, and May Amelia. May Amelia was named for her mother, but we allus called her Love, 'cause she was allus so kind to everybody. The Fitzpatrick, Major Andrews, and Baldwin darkies was called "free niggers" 'cause our masters has respect for them.

My old master was a doctor, but he worked 'bout five hundred acres of land and owned 'bout eighty-five darkies. The darkies lived in log quarters. Some of them had them "son-of-a-gun" beds made of planks pegged to the wall, and some of them didn't. We wore bach'lor brogan shoes and white, red, yellow, blue and striped Lowell clothes made on the place. We allus had most anything we wanted to eat. I's seed long rows of hogs hanging in the yard at killing time. My mother allus said she had a heap better time in slavery than after she left the Baldwins.

All the hands was up and in the fields by daylight. Nobody laid in bed up in the morning like folks do today. Dr. Baldwin allus had a fifty-gallon barrel of whiskey on the place. He kept a demijohn of whiskey on the front porch all the time for the darkies to get a drink on the way to the field in the morning. You never heard of nobody getting drunk then. Master's brother-in-law, Lewis Brantley, was overseer, but he never kicked, and cuffed, and beat the darkies. He give us a light brushing when we needed it. The darkies was allowed to go most anywhere they wanted to if they got a permit. They had big dances on 'joining places but I never 'tended them. We had play parties on the place on Saturday night and played "Red Morocco Shoes and Stockings" and games like that.

The first work I done was hoeing. I went to work in the field when I was 'bout nine years old, but Mistress took me out of the field and put me in the house. My mama was a house woman . . . the weaver, milker, and nurse.

I was bo'n to see ghosts, but times is changed, and you don't see any now. Some of the darkies was allus seeing ghosts in slavery time. They had all kinds of shapes and was all sizes, but I never seed any after I got grown.

I went to school three months in my life. That was the first year of Abe Lincoln's war. A Yankee named Old Man Mills run a school on the Sledge place. I quit to work in the field. If I had stayed with him I might have been somewhere now. There was a church on the Sledge place, too, but we didn't go much.

I 'members when the war started, and when it ceased. My

father went to the war with Lewis Brantley. Dr. Baldwin let him go with his brother-in-law to wait on him, but he had to fit [fight] 'fore it was over. My folks stayed on with the Baldwins three years after the war ceased and moved to the Haggerty place.

I 'members seeing them Ku Kluxing the darkies right after the war. I's seed big bunches of darkies with their heads tied up pass our place going to Marshall to report the Ku Kluxers to the Progee Marshall. Just 'bout the close of the war I got hold of a song I thought was pretty and was allus singing it, but didn't know what it meant. It went like this:

> Old river ain't you sorry as you can be.
> We go marching home, we go marching home
> 'Cause we hung Jeff Davis to a sour-apple tree.

I went through the house singing it one day, and Mistress heard me and hollered, "Lucy, hush your singing that song." I had a good voice, and she allus like to hear me sing so I didn't know 'til I was grown why she made me hush sing it. I found out it was a Yankee soldier song they sung after the surrender at the Battle of Mansfield.

I knows lots 'bout old Colonel Haggerty's widow. I's heard my master and Grandma tell 'bout her. My master was the doctor, and the Haggerty place jined our place. Old Widow Haggerty was an Indian, and her first husband was chief of the Caddo Indians when they lived on Caddo Lake. Grandma Barbara told us that Widow Haggerty's first husband broke a treaty with the Indians and betrayed them to the Americans, and he and his wife hid out in a cave on Caddo Lake. His wife slipped out and got him food and water. One day when she was away, the Indians found him and took him away, and she never seed him no more. They say the Indians scalped him like they done white folks. After the Indians killed him, his wife married Old Colonel Haggerty. He was a gambler and went off on a gambling spree and was killed. He left his widow a lot of property and 'bout three hundred slaves. My grandma said she kept a Negro woman chained to a loom for a year. My master said that when Widow Haggerty knowed the slaves was going to be freed that she poisoned lot of her darkies and buried them at night. I 'members when we heard her darkies crying and moaning at one and two o'clock in the morning for their dead ones. That Widow Haggerty was sumpin'. When my folks lived on the Haggerty place, I's been right to the cave where they say her first husband hid from the Indians.

I 'members when the big boats come to Port Caddo and to Jefferson. I seed the *Mattie Stephens* boat the day after it burned and killed sixty people. Me and Anthony Thomas went to Marshall and married the day 'fore it burned. We come home the next day and went to Port Caddo where they brought the hull to the shore. That was on February 12, 1869, and I was eighteen years old. That ship burning is another way I calculate how old I is. The ship was on the way to Jefferson from New Orleans when it burned, and had 'bout a hundred people on it.

I's seed darkies by the droves going to Marshall to be on the jury. Then they had to be crazy to get off it. I had a uncle called on the jury. He was busy in the crops and didn't want to go. He stuffed his clothes with rags like he was disfigured, and when they 'zammended [examined] him they ask him if he knowed the day of the month and he said, "Yes, sah, it am the sixty-seventh." I laugh at him after then when he wanted on it, and they wouldn't let him.

William Adams

William Adams, age ninety-three, was born in slavery, with no opportunity for an education, except three months in a public school. He has taught himself to read and to write. His lifelong ambition has been to become master of the supernatural powers that he believes to exist. He is now well known among southwestern Negroes for his faith in the occult.

You want to know and talk about the power the people tells you I has. Well, sit down here, right there in that chair, befo' we'uns starts. I gits some ice water and then we'uns can discuss the subject. I wants to explain it clearly so you's can understand.

I's born a slave, ninety-three years ago, so of course I's 'members the war period. Like all the other slaves I has no chance for education. Three months am the total time I's spent going to school. I teached myself to read and write. I's anxious to learn to read so I could study and find out about many things. That, I has done.

There am lots of folks, and educated ones, too, what says

William Adams

we'uns believes in superstition. Well, it's 'cause they don't understand. 'Member the Lawd, in some of His ways, can be mysterious. The Bible says so. There am some things the Lawd wants all folks to know. Some thinks just the chosen few to know 'bout some of the Lawd's laws. Ain't superstition if some other person understands and believes in such.

There is some born to sing, some born to preach, and some born to know the signs. There is some born under the power of the devil and have the power to put injury and misery on people, and some born under the power of the Lawd for to do good and overcome the evil power. Now, that produces two forces, like fire and water. The evil forces starts the fire, and I has the water forces to put the fire out.

How I learnt such? Well, I's done learnt it. It comes to me. When the Lawd gives such power to a person, it just comes to 'em. It am forty years ago now when I's first fully realize that I has the power. However, I allus int'rested in the workin's of the signs. I hears them talk about what happens to folks 'cause a spell was put on 'em. The old folks in them days know more about the signs that the Lawd uses to reveal His laws than the folks of today. It am also true of the cullud folks in Africa, they native land. Some of the folks laughs at their beliefs and says it am superstition, but it am knowin' how the Lawd reveals His laws.

Now, let me tell you of something I's seen. What am seen, can't be doubted. It happens when I's a young man and befo' I's realize that I's one that am chosen for to show the power. A mule had cut his leg so bad that him am bleedin' to death, and they couldn't stop it. An old cullud man live near there. He comes over and passes his hand over the cut. Befo' long the bleedin' stop, and that's the power of the Lawd workin' through that nigger, that's all it am.

I knows 'bout a woman that lost her mind. The doctors say

it was caused from a tumor in the head. They took an x-ray picture, but there's no tumor. They gives up and says it's a peculiar case. That woman was took to one with the power of the good spirit, and he says it's a peculiar case for them that don't understand. This am a case of the evil spell. Two days after, the woman have her mind back.

They's lots of those kind of cases the ord'nary person never hear about. You hear of the case the doctors can't understand, nor will they 'spond to treatment. That am 'cause of the evil spell that am on the persons.

'Bout special persons bein' chose for to show the power, read you's Bible. It says in the book of Mark, third chapter: "And He ordained twelve, that they should be with Him, that He might send them forth to preach and to have the power to heal the sick and to cast out devils." If it wasn't no evil in people, why does the Lawd say cast out such? And in the fifth chapter of James, it further say: "If any am sick, let him call the elders. Let them pray over him. The prayers of faith shall save him." There 'tis again, faith, that am what counts.

When I tells that I seen many persons given up to die, and then a man with the power comes and saves such person, then it's not for people to say it am superstition to believe in the power.

Don't forget—the agents of the devil have the power of evil. They can put misery of every kind on people. They can make trouble with the work, and with the business, with the fam'ly, and the health. So folks must be on the watch all the time. Folks has business trouble 'cause the evil power have control of 'em. They has the evil power cast out and save the business. There am a man in Waco that come to see me 'bout that. He say to me everything he try to do in the last six months turned out wrong. It starts with him losin' his pocketbook with fifty dollars in it. He buys a carload of hay, and it catch fire, and he lost all of it. He spends two hundred dollars advertisin' a three-day sale, and it begin to rain, so he lost money. It sho' am the evil power.

"Well," he say, "That am the way it go, so I comes to you."

I says to him, "It's the evil power that have you control, and we'uns shall cause it to be cast out." It's done, and he has no more trouble.

You wants to know if persons with the power for good can be successful in castin' out devils in all cases? Well, I answers that, yes and no. They can in every case if the affected person have the faith. If the party not have enough faith, then it am a failure.

Wearin' the coin for protection 'gainst the evil power? That am simple. Lots of folks wears such, and they uses mixtures that am sprinkled in the house and such. That am a question of faith. If they has the true faith in such, it works. Otherwise, it won't.

Some folks won't think for a minute of goin' without lodestone, or the salt and pepper mixture in the little sack tied 'round they neck. Some wears the silver coin tied 'round they neck. All such am for to keep away the effect of the evil power. When one have the faith in such and they acc'dently [accidently] lose they charm, they sho' am miserable.

An old darky that has faith in lodestone for the charm told me the experience he has in Atlanta once. He carryin' brick, and the first thing he does is drop some on he foot. The next thing, his foot slips, and him starts up the ladder, and him and the brick drop to the ground. It am lucky for him it wasn't far. Just a sprain ankle, and the boss sends him home for the day. He gits on the streetcar and when the conductor call for the fare, Rufus reaches for he money but he lose it or forgits it at home. The conductor say he let him pay next time and asks where he live. Rufus tells him, and he say, "Why, nigger, you is on the wrong car." That cause Rufus to walk further with the lame foot than if he started walkin' in the first place. He thinks there must be something wrong with he charm, and he look for it, and it gone! Sho 'nough, it am lost. He think, "Here I sits all day, and I won't make another move 'til I gits the lodestone. When the chillens come from school I sends them to the drugstore for some of the stone and gits fixed."

Now, now, I's been waitin' for that one 'bout the black cat crossin' the road, and sho' 'nough, it comes. Let me ask you one. How many people can you find that likes to have the black cat cross in front of 'em? That's right, no one likes that. Let this old cullud person informs you that it am sho' the bad luck sign. It is sign of bad luck ahead, so turn back. Stop what you's doin'.

I's tellin' you of two of many cases of failure to took warnin' from the black cat. I known a man call Miller. His wife and him am takin' an auto ride and that black cat cross the road, and he cussed a little and goes on. Then it not long 'til he turns the corner, and his wife falls out of the car durin' the turn. When he goes back and picks her up, she am dead.

Another fellow, call Brown, was a-ridin' hossback and a black cat crosses the path, but he drives on. Well, it's not long 'til he hoss stumble and throws him off. The fall breaks his leg, so take a warnin'—don't overlook the black cat. That am a warnin'.